NEVADA

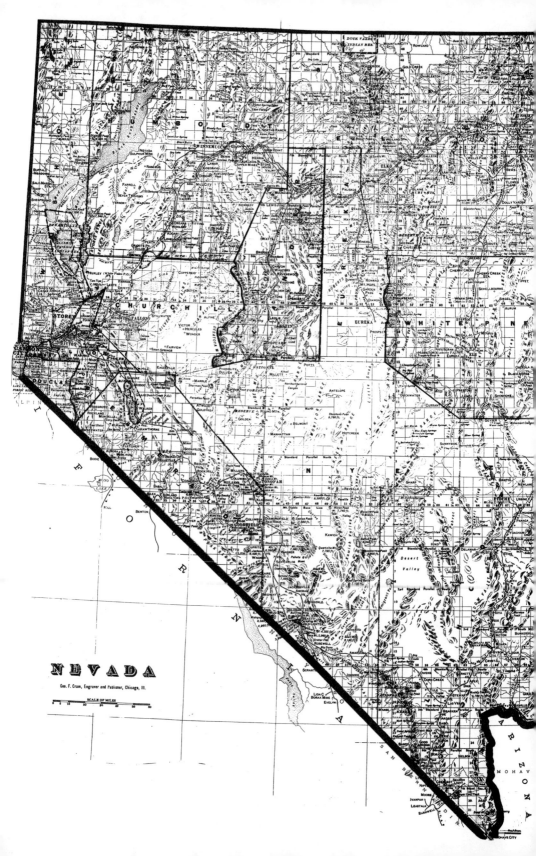

NEVADA

Geo. F. Cram, Engraver and Publisher, Chicago, Ill.

SCALE OF MILES

NEVADA
Lost Mines
& Buried
Treasures

by
Douglas McDonald

Illustrations by Roy E. Purcell

published by Stanley W. Paher

Nevada Publications

Box 15444
Las Vegas, Nev. 89114

Something hidden. Go and find it.
Go and look behind the Ranges —
Something lost behind the Ranges.
Lost and waiting for you. Go!

Rudyard Kipling
The Explorer

About the Author

Douglas McDonald has spent most of his life in Nevada. He has written several historical articles and another book, *Julia Bulette and the Red Light Ladies of Nevada*. He has collected various Nevada historical items, including postal cancellations, coins and bank notes, books, and photographs. He is currently working on a book about Virginia City, where he presently resides.

Illustrations

On the cover is Roy Purcell's magnificent etching "Forgotten Dreams" which depicts the shaft headframe of one of the mines of the Clifford district of central Nye County. All of the 17 interior illustrations are line sketches drawn by Purcell, who has been a contributor to many books and articles on the desert Southwest.

The map on the back cover is of the "Gold Hill Front Lodes" on the Comstock Lode, from the promotional booklet *Statement and Reports concerning the Uncle Sam Senior and Gold Canon Silver Lodes, in Nevada*, published in 1865. Some of the author's Carson City minted coins are added to the photograph.

Several of the photographs and the line drawing of Austin are from the collections of the author and publisher. Other photo credits are as follows:

Dorothy Jennings collection, 122. Nevada Historical Society collections, 38, 48, 59, 63, 64, 69, 73, 74, 75, 85, 88, 97; Robert Allen collection, 15; Effie Mona Mack collection, 10. Marilyn Newton photo, 78. Effie Read collection, 29. C. W. West photo, 56.

Nevada Publications has issued more than two dozen books on the southwest involving travel, ghost towns, mining and transportation history. All are highly pictorial with maps and other aids to assist the reader. Write for complete catalog.

INTRODUCTION

The American West, a legendary country in itself, abounds with a multitude of tales and legends in which Westerners boast, fool each other, or generally entertain themselves. Folklore is a part of everyone who has grown up in the mining and desert country. The stories have at least a small influence on the lives of all, and recently Easterners and Europeans have begun to take pride in the lore of the West. Nevada history is especially enriched with many of these stories of forgotten treasures and lost mines.

This book includes Nevada's best treasure legends, told as faithfully as possible. They have been gathered from published volumes of history, old pioneer accounts, personal interviews, and especially from early-day magazines and newspapers. Some were also collected in bar rooms, around campfires, and at poker tables.

Where possible I have verified the details of these stories, particularly the topography, place names, etc., but in many instances it is impossible to authenticate the various points of a tale. As was stated many years ago:

"I dare not say how true 't may be—
I tell the tale as 'twas told to me."

One thing which most of the accounts have in common is a lack of detail. Thus it is often very nearly impossible to distinguish fact from fiction. Far too much misinformation has been perpetuated about many of Nevada's lost mines, principally since it is easier to embellish an existing tale than to try to authenticate it. I have endeavored to furnish as much information as possible about each story, thus allowing the reader to draw his own inferences and conclusions.

While this collection of stories represents every tale or lead that I have been able to run down in the past ten years, there are certainly some that I have missed. By the same token, some reader may have information which disproves or modifies some of these legends. Anyone with additions, corrections, or further information of any sort is asked to please contact me in care of the publisher.

Through this program of research, two stories of long standing have recently been proven false: "Manuel Gonzales' Buried Loot" and "Hank Knight's Lost Cave of Gold." Serious treasure hunting buffs might well note the absence of the story of the 1916 stage robbery at Jarbidge, in which an express shipment was stolen and buried. I have it on good authority that the missing strongbox has been found by a well-known California treasure hunter and all of its contents recovered. Good hunting!

—Douglas McDonald

Table of Contents

Boak-West photo of the "BY. FOGLE"
rock in Forty Mile Canyon.

1 LOST BREYFOGLE MINE

The famous tale of the lost Breyfogle mine has been in the public eye for more than a hundred years. From the first writings about it in the mid-1860's, through all the claims that it had been found in the early 1900's, to the modern-day accounts of this elusive vein of gold, no one has been able to prove with certainty that any one version of the tale is true.

Several southern Nevada candidates for the lost Breyfogle mine have been brought forward in the Chispa mine, the Johnnie mine, the Round Mountain diggings, the Montgomery mine at Bullfrog, the flush mines around Goldfield, and even the lost Pegleg mine. There are even variations of the discoverer's first name—it has been reported as Louie, Jacob, or Charles in various stories.

The first known reference of Charles C. Breyfogle in the West lists him as being elected Assessor of Alameda County, California, in 1854. He remained in various public offices in that county until at least 1858, and afterwards he probably joined the rush to the Comstock, although there is no documentation of this. It is known, though, that mining fever hit hard in 1863, when he took part in the stampede to "Reese River" in Lander County.

Most Breyfogle researchers claim that he was a blacksmith in the newly founded town of Austin, but an eyewitness later wrote that Breyfogle worked in David Buel's quartz mill at Big Creek, 16 miles south of Austin, almost from the time he arrived there. Although gainfully employed as a mill hand, his first love was prospecting for gold and silver. At every available opportunity he packed his horses and roamed the sage-covered deserts of central Nevada.

At that time, J. F. Triplett worked in a livery stable in Austin where Breyfogle kept his animals. He often talked with the prospector both before and after his searches for ore. An account written by Triplett, concerning the journey on which Breyfogle made his famous find, is related in an obscure volume entitled *Annual Edition Reno Evening Gazette, 1904-05*. Triplett says, " . . . when he started on his last and most perilous trip he outfitted at Austin. I was working in a livery stable at the time, and saddled his horses, adjusted his packs and hung a small canvas bag over his shoulder when he started. I was still at the stable when the old gentleman returned and know that he brought back the same saddles and animals that he started with and that a man's hat would hold all of the ore that he brought in."

Triplett told all that he knew of Breyfogle's habits, stating that it was the prospector's custom to stop wherever there was good water and check the surrounding area. After he was satisfied that there was nothing of value in the vicinity, he would move on until he again found water, then resume prospecting.

Nevada's most famous lost mine legend began on just such an occasion in 1863. While away from his camp looking for ore, he left his horses at the foot of a hill. Ascending it he found a rich quartz deposit. He became so excited over his discovery that he completely forgot about his horses, spending most of the day exploring and taking samples. When he returned for them in the late afternoon, they had disappeared.

Breyfogle knew that he had to recover them and so he followed their tracks until dark. He spent the night in the open sagebrush and resumed his searching as soon as there was enough light to track by. The day passed with the horses' prints being obscured by the wind and terrain, the trail finally vanishing. His water was gone, and the heat was dazing him so much that he soon had no idea of where he was or what he was doing. Evidently he blacked out, for when he awoke he found himself in a camp of friendly Shoshones. His horses were also grazing nearby and Breyfogle knew he was saved.

As neither Breyfogle nor the Indians could communicate with each other, he had no idea how long he had been there or where they had found him. As soon as he had recovered enough to be able to travel, he headed back to Austin. Triplett later wrote, "When he returned he was in a sad plight, his head being fearfully blistered from the hot sun."

Despite his ordeal, the prospector knew he had found a gold mine. Ten days after his return to Austin he had convinced his employer, Dave Buel, to organize a search party and return to stake the claim. He had no trouble locating the Indian camp where he had been rescued, but try as he would he simply could not remember which way he had come while tracking his horses. Buel's party so exhausted their animals in looking for the gold that they returned to Austin with just one mule, since all the rest had died in the desert.

In the following year Breyfogle made two more trips in search of his lost gold, each sponsored by other men, and both proved to be failures. In 1865, he finally gave up the search and returned to his former home in California. His labors and his age had taken their toll, and he died that same year.

A piece of the Breyfogle ore was supposedly saved and displayed some years afterwards in Austin. This alone was enough to send scores of prospectors out on the trail of the lost mine, and in the decades following the discovery numerous parties of men searched all over southwestern Nevada for the "Lost Breyfogle." The story spread far afield, but with each retelling some of the facts and even the dates were changed until by the 1920's no one really knew what the true story had been. Also, by that time, a number of new mines had been located which had ore similar to Breyfogle's and were near the vicinity in which he might have made his discovery.

Many people claimed the "Breyfogle" simply had to have been found since there was no proof to the contrary. Then in the early 1930's an old prospector named Roscoe Wright, out of Goldfield, found an unusual rock formation in Forty Mile Canyon east of Beatty. The sandstone formation was striking by itself, but more important was the carving on it. In large block letters the rock read "BY. FOGLE 1863."

Hoping that this might be a lead to the elusive Breyfogle ore, Wright called on mineralogist C. C. Boak and Dr. C. W. West, President of the Nevada State Park Commission. Together the three men returned to Forty Mile Canyon and photographed the rock and its inscription. Wright prospected the area thereafter but found no trace of the rich gold ore.

It seems reasonable that if a man had made a fabulous find and was near death, that he would try to leave a marker behind. And, if that man was weak and dazed from heat and thirst, it would seem that his note would be brief. Thus, "BY. FOGLE" might be short for Breyfogle, but at this time no one can be certain.

At any rate, if the rich quartz is still unfound and is somewhere in the vicinity of the rock in Forty Mile Canyon, it may take some time to find it. Since 1951 that area has been part of the Las Vegas Bombing and Gunnery Range and only authorized personnel are allowed within its bounds. Whether the ore is still lost or not, its story remains one of central Nevada's favorite topics of campfire and saloon conversation.

Another photo of the rock, taken in 1941 by Robert Allen of the Nevada State Highway Department. This view shows more of the surrounding terrain in the canyon.

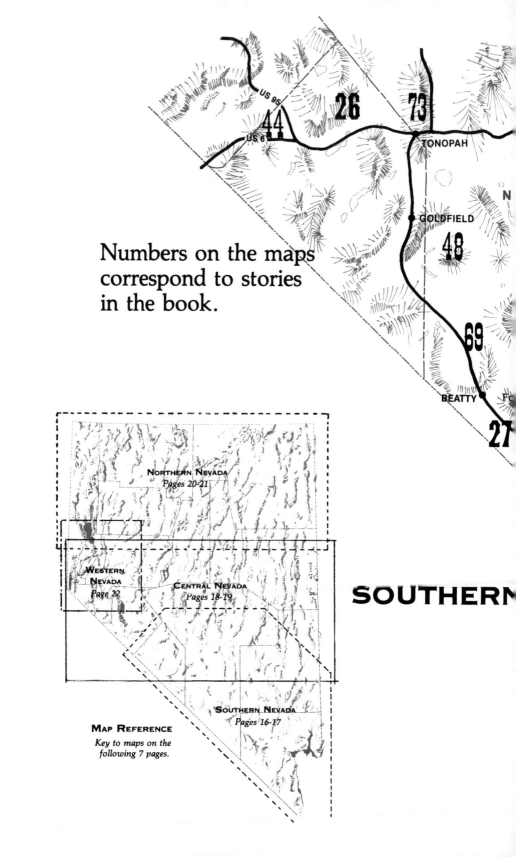

Numbers on the maps
correspond to stories
in the book.

US 95

US 6

44

26

73

TONOPAH

GOLDFIELD

48

N

69

BEATTY   F

27

NORTHERN NEVADA
Pages 20-21

WESTERN
NEVADA
Page 22

CENTRAL NEVADA
Pages 18-19

SOUTHERN

SOUTHERN NEVADA
Pages 16-17

MAP REFERENCE
*Key to maps on the
following 7 pages.*

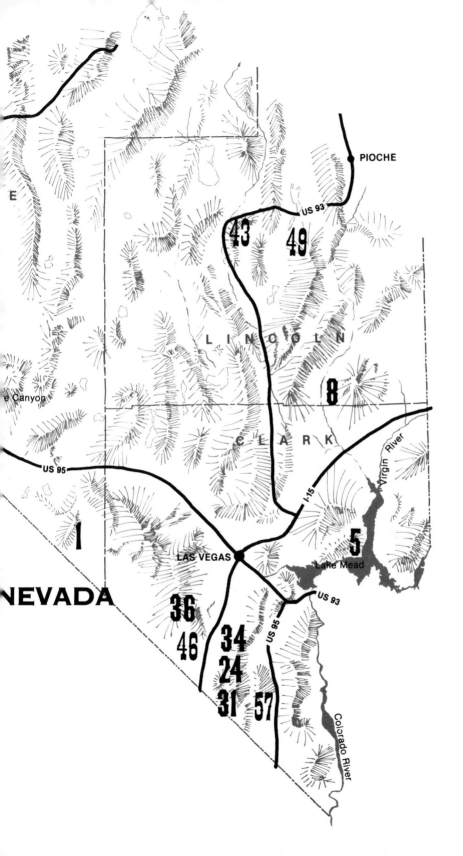

PIOCHE

US 93

E

43 **49**

e Canyon

L I N C O L N

8

C L A R K

Virgin River

I-15

US 95

NEVADA

1

LAS VEGAS

5

Lake Mead

36

US 93

46 **34**

US 95

24

31 **57**

Colorado River

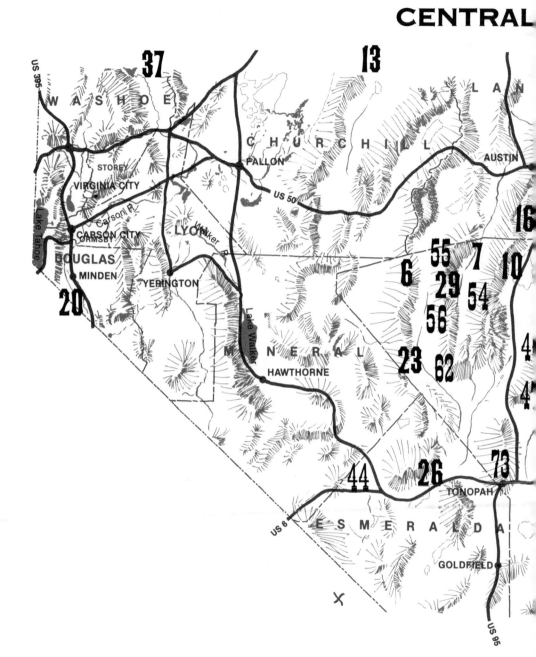

NEVADA

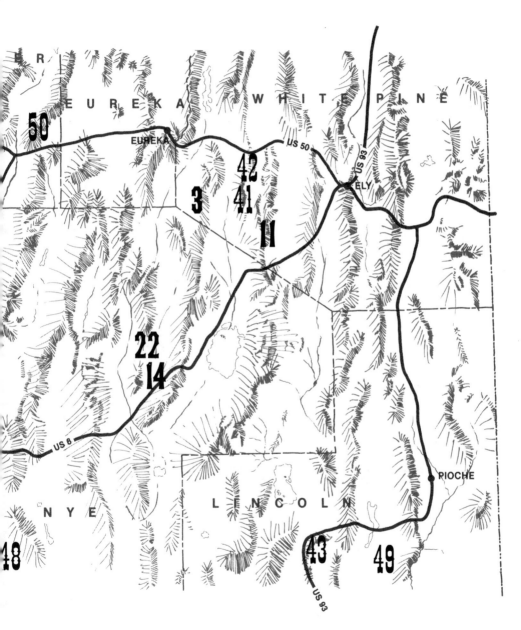

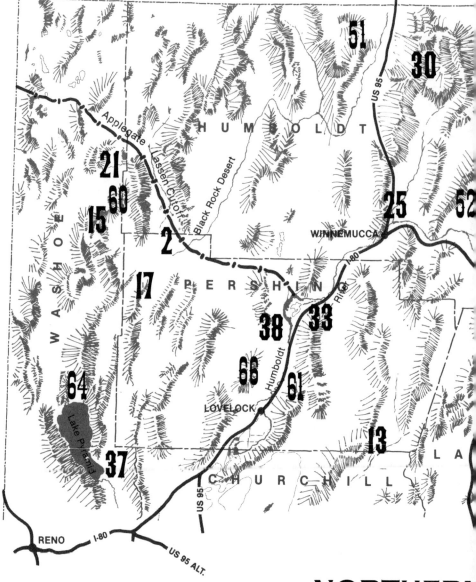

NORTHERN

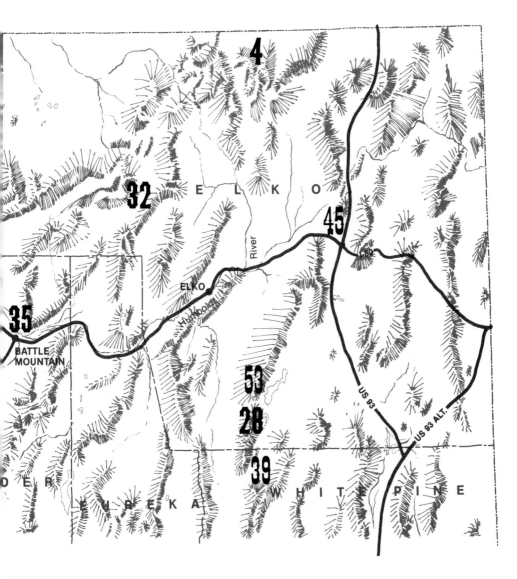

NEVADA

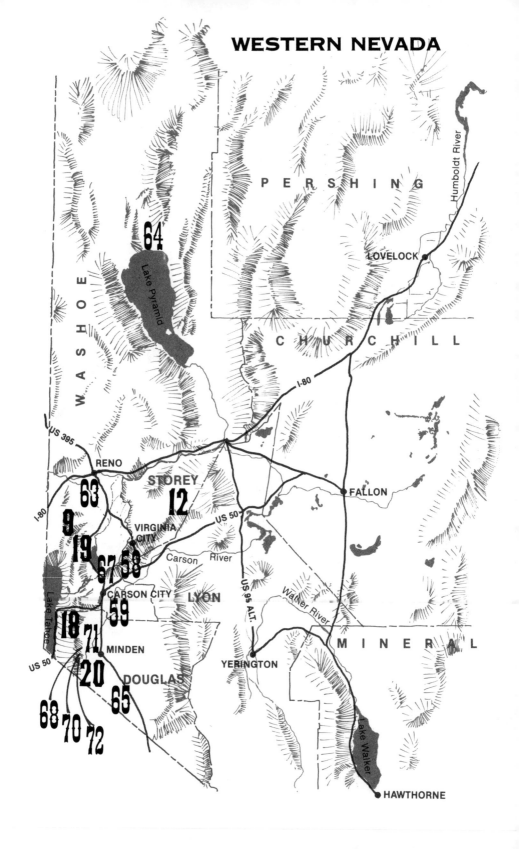

WESTERN NEVADA

2. LOST HARDIN SILVER

While stories of lost mines are plentiful, often creating legends that are slow in dying, it is unusual when one tale of elusive ore leads to a full-scale mining rush and the creation of a boom town. Such was the case with the lost Hardin silver and the short-lived mining camp of Hardin City in the desolate Black Rock Desert of northwestern Nevada.

James Allen Hardin came west from somewhere in the eastern states, joining a wagon train headed for Oregon in the spring of 1849. He crossed the plains and Rockies on the Emigrant Trail, and took the Applegate-Lassen Cut-Off from the Humboldt River. The train crossed the Black Rock Desert, rounded Black Rock Point, and finally camped to rest for awhile at Double Hot Springs.

As the emigrants were short on almost everything by this time, especially food, Hardin volunteered to go hunting in the Black Rock Range. He took John Lambert with him to scout the foothills for something to fill the larders. When they were about three or four miles north of Double Hot Springs they crossed a dry sandy wash where something bright caught Hardin's eye. He stopped to investigate and found chunks of metal scattered throughout the sand in the wash. Thinking it might be lead, and being short of bullets, Hardin and Lambert took some of the shiny rock with them. Finding no game that day, the two men returned to camp. Hardin borrowed an oven that night to cast most of the metal he had found into bullets. He kept one chunk of the ore for use later and carried it with him when the train moved on to Oregon.

Hardin eventually settled in Petaluma, California, where he worked as a carpenter. He had forgotten all about the lead he had found until a neighbor of his, an assayer, happened to see it in his shop one day. The assayer asked if he could test the rock; the result showed that Hardin had years before cast lead bullets containing quite a high percentage of silver.

Hardin immediately began assembling a small expedition to the Black Rock area to stake a claim on the ravine. The *Petaluma Journal* of July 9, 1858, chronicled the party's leaving, " . . . they go in search of what they believe to be an immense deposit of silver ore."

Bleak and forbodding, Black Rock Point sticks out into the utterly barren Black Rock Desert.

Try as he might, Hardin could not locate the silver again. His group spent the summer of 1858 hunting for it, finally giving up when cold weather set in. The following spring they were all back and others joined in the search. No one could locate any trace of the silver. The Paiute War which broke out just south of the Black Rock in 1860 put an end to most of the prospecting in that country. It is not likely that Hardin returned to look for his silver during the next five years.

Then early in 1866 a man from the Honey Lake area of California discovered a ledge that was immediately thought to be the lost silver lode. The word spread like wildfire, and prospectors flocked to the Black Rock Desert to get in on the strike. The camp of Hardin City sprang up near the mines, named in honor of the original discoverer.

A small batch of Black Rock ore was worked which yielded significant returns in both gold and silver. When the news was released, the rush intensified. The *Humboldt Register*, March 24, 1866, reported, "When you see a man sitting in front of a roll of blankets and a frying pan, and behind a Henry rifle, you need not ask him where he is going—he is 'going to Black Rock or burst.' "

Everyone talked about the mines, and during 1866 the Black Rock rush was "all the go," but for some reason only certain shipments of ore gave any returns. Others brought no results at all. Dall's Mill in Washoe Valley was the one that received most of the ore for processing, and it turned out to be the only one which yielded returns on the ore. Other wagonloads were sent to a mill on the Humboldt River, but word came back that the rock was worthless. In spite of this seeming contradiction, the rush continued and Hardin City expanded. A post office and a few businesses opened while two mills were built to avoid sending the ore miles away for refining. The year 1866 was a good year for Black Rock.

The true test of the Hardin City ores came the following year, when the mills there began operating in earnest. This time every test showed the ore to be barren of both silver and gold and completely valueless. An expert assayer was called in and, after viewing the situation, claimed that a different reduction process was needed. Modifications were made in one mill, but even then it failed to produce anything. By the middle of 1868 everything had been abandoned and Hardin City passed into history.

Double Hot Springs, located about midway between Black Rock Point and Hardin City, was a noted landmark on the Applegate-Lassen Cut-Off. Although the water here is hot and highly mineralized, it still became a welcomed rest spot after crossing the completely dry Black Rock Desert.

The Calico Hills section of the Black Rock
Range, due east of the site of Hardin City. Somewhere in these hills Hardin's lost silver still
lies hidden.

26

Ruins of the Evans Mill, one of the last remaining vestiges of Hardin City.

Eventually the story came out that the only reason values had been found in the ore at Dall's Mill was because of the process used there. The mill pans had not been cleaned thoroughly before the Black Rock ore was run, and the alkali in the rock picked up the gold and silver left in the pans. Any values merely came from the batches of Comstock ore which had been run previously.

Rock foundations, an arrastra, and depressions where buildings once stood are still visible at Hardin City. The only thing that its failure proves is that Hardin's silver had not been relocated. For the past hundred years numerous adventurers have continued to cover the Black Rock area in search of it. True believers insist that the silver is still in an unknown dry wash, but that it has been covered by the sand and dirt of later cloudbursts. Hardin found it once. As the desert terrain changes continuously, someone may find it again.

William Pogue, the "miser" of Little Smokey Valley, in front of his station, c. 1910.

3. POGUE STATION TREASURE

In southwestern White Pine County, on an old stage road along the west slope of the Pancake Mountains, lie the ruins of Pogue's Station. Of this once busy stage and freight stop, little remains except adobe and stone walls and the lingering legend of William Pogue, the "miser" of Little Smokey Valley.

Early in the 1890's, when travel in the area south of Eureka was still heavy, Pogue located a spring on the main road south into Nye County. He realized that travelers had to stop there as it was the only water between Eureka and Duckwater, so he constructed a station, horse barn, corrals, and some outbuildings. He enlarged the spring and dug a well for easy access to the water.

Pogue profited by selling meals, water, and lodgings for travelers to stay the night. He secured contracts to supply feed and water to stage lines and then convinced Nye County officials to pay him for maintaining the road in his area. He even found time to do a little prospecting, claiming that he had found a mine "back in the hills" which paid fairly well. It seemed everything he did made money, his yearly income estimated at being around $25,000.

Pogue's Station as it appeared in 1966. Today even this ruin has been reduced to a pile of rubble.

However, the old man was noted for his frugality. He never took vacations, only leaving his station long enough to make infrequent trips to Eureka for supplies. He was never robbed and he sent no money to anyone. Those who knew him believed that he was a miser, stashing his money away somewhere near his station.

For more than twenty years old man Pogue operated this way, ever making money. Then on May 15, 1915, during a time when traffic was slow, a passer-by found him lying helpless on the floor of his house. He had evidently suffered a stroke and had lain there for several days. The traveler made him as comfortable as possible, then hurried to the nearest ranch for help. Word was sent to Duckwater, and on the following morning Ralph Irwin drove his car up to take the ill station-keeper to the county hospital at Eureka. Completely paralyzed from the waist down, Pogue was

in very serious condition. He never recovered from the effects of the stroke and died three days later on the morning of the 19th.

An examination of his personal belongings furnished a little information about his early life. He had apparently been born in Greenville, Tennessee, 75 years earlier, and had one living relative, a sister in Illinois. Further searching failed to turn up any trace of his wealth, which was then thought to be about $200,000.

The story that his station was the site of buried money spread around the country, luring treasure hunters on a search for it. In 1917, two Duckwater residents found some coins hidden under a rock, and in 1936, prospector John Hoyt found $11 in a hole in the station compound. Although the place has been thoroughly searched time and time again, no other money has ever been found.

Today the station is in ruins, since treasure hunters have completely destroyed the buildings in their careless quest. The station yard is full of shallow pits and low mounds marking old excavations, yet the treasure must still be hidden somewhere near the station. Perhaps modern electronic equipment may some day uncover the spot where it lies. But on the other hand, the old-timers like Pogue were cagey characters, and the ghost of the old man may laugh forever at the unsuccessful searchers.

JARBIDGE NEV.
© BY W EYLE 1917. K17

4. LOST SHEEPHERDER MINE

The wild country of northeastern Nevada, surrounding the isolated gold town of Jarbidge, is a country full of strange legends. Even the name Jarbidge is a corruption of the Shoshone word for a giant Indian-eating devil, but none of these tales matches the strange legend of the lost Sheepherder mine and of the men who died on its trail.

Prospectors had been in the Jarbidge vicinity since the late 1870's, although little gold was ever found in those early years. Then in about 1890 a prospector known as Ross made a trip into the area. He intended to prospect until winter set in and then return to more civilized climates, but in late summer he stumbled upon some very rich gold float. He was still trying to locate its source when the first snow of the season began to fall, so he hurriedly stuck his pick and shovel in the ground to mark the spot. While starting out of the mountains Ross ran into a sheep camp owned by an Elko County rancher, John Pence. The herder, Ishman by name, invited the prospector to share his supper and spend the night.

Jarbidge in 1917, at the peak of its prosperity. Rugged mountains and steep canyons characterize the country in this area, making prospecting difficult.

For some reason which has never been determined, Ross told Ishman about the float he had been tracing all summer. He described the terrain and landmarks and even told him of the pick and shovel in the ground marking the highest reach that he had traced the ore. He also said that Ishman should consider the gold his if anything should happen to him and he did not return within the year.

The following spring, while the snow was melting from the mountain meadows, Ishman returned with his sheep. As rapidly as possible, he started hunting for the landmarks which would lead him to the gold. He eventually found the pick and shovel stuck in the ground, and nearby he found a human skeleton. He could never establish whether the bones were Ross', but it is known that the prospector never again returned to the area.

It took nearly the entire summer for Ishman to find the ledge, but when he did it was well worth it. The trail of float had led him to a cropping of rock that was shot through with gold. Before any exploratory work could be done, though, winter began to set in again. Ishman picked up a few pounds of the ore and covered all traces of the outcrop. He carefully covered his tracks while returning down the slopes. As soon as camp was broken and the sheep were bunched, he started back for the home ranch.

During the winter Ishman told his employer all about the discovery and showed him the ore samples. Pence immediately had them assayed, which excited both men over the richness they returned. Together they planned how best to develop the ore body and impatiently waited out the remainder of the winter. When spring finally came, they both headed up to the area of the find. Excitement spurred them on and they pushed as fast as possible up the steep canyons and hillsides, believing that they were getting ever closer to the gold. But the strain proved too much for the old sheepherder and Ishman suddenly collapsed, dying a few days later without regaining consciousness. Ishman had given his boss a fairly good idea of where the gold was, but despite many searches Pence could never locate it. He spent summer after summer grubstaking prospectors to hunt for it, but no one came any closer than he had been at the time of Ishman's death.

In late 1908, D. A. Bourne struck rich gold ore on the banks of the Jarbidge River. A spectacular mining rush ensued that brought about the town of Jarbidge. The ore was extremely highgrade, leading a number of people to believe that the Jarbidge discovery was perhaps the lost Sheepherder mine. Someone, though, took the time to analyze and compare the ore samples Ishman found with those from Jarbidge and stated that the "Sheepherder" croppings had to be some five miles or so from the townsite and higher on the mountain slopes.

Most agree that it is still lost, but one storyteller recently claimed that he and an aged prospector from Reno had found the lost mine in 1932. They supposedly took out more than $23,000 in one summer, shipped it to the San Francisco Mint, and split the profit. Taking his share in cash, the bearer of this tale boarded a ship bound for Australia where he eventually made a fortune in opals.

In 1965, he thought to look up the old prospector he had worked with near Jarbidge and returned to San Francisco where he had left him 33 years earlier. Once there, he learned that his partner had died during the winter of 1932-33. Believing that no one had been to the discovery site since, he gave rough directions to the long abandoned workings. He stated it was located north of Jarbidge, over the ridge toward the Bruneau River, and about a quarter mile below a tall rock peak on the ridge.

The gold is there, according to at least three men who claim to have seen it. But as anyone knows who has ever been in that country, the canyons and mountains are among the steepest and roughest in the state. Mules and "shank's mare" are the only practical means of transportation. If anyone is going to find the lost Sheepherder mine, it will take an enormous amount of luck, work, and capital. But the story goes on—and so do the prospectors.

5 SECOND LOST PEGLEG MINE

Among the most famous lost gold mine stories in the history of the Southwest is the legend of Pegleg Smith and his lost placer deposit. For more than 150 years men searched for it, books have been written about it, and some people actually have claimed to have found it. It has been reported as being in either Arizona or California and at least one man claims to have been mining it secretly for the past decade. Whatever the story, Pegleg's "varnish-coated" nuggets have been searched for over a period of many years, yet few people know that he was instrumental in another placer gold deposit which was found and lost in southern Nevada.

In 1827, when beaver trapping was a big business all over the West, Smith joined a party of mountain men under Ewing Young who set out to work the Colorado River for beaver. The group reached a Mohave Indian village just east of where Needles, California, is today and promptly got into trouble over some local squaws. After a brief fight, the mountaineers managed to get out of the camp and continue north.

The Indians, though, had taken offense at the treatment they had suffered, a group of them harassing the men continuously as they traveled along. Finally the trappers counterattacked one night and wiped out the band of Mohaves while they slept. With this hindrance out of the way, they were quite free to return to their explorations for beaver.

On the north side of the Colorado River, two miles east of where it then met the Virgin River, the men camped for a few days to rest and explore the area. During this time another trapper, Dutch George, arrived into camp with a handful of nuggets. Smith looked them over, stated that they were natural copper, and proceeded to use them for casting bullets. Weeks later, when the Colorado was found to be unfavorable for trapping beaver,

Smith and a few others broke away from the main party and worked their way north toward the Great Salt Lake, forgetting all about the "copper" they had found.

This idea of the nuggets being copper was quite plausible to Smith. At that time the only large mine operating in the Southwest, the Santa Rita in New Mexico, was producing copper nuggets in much the same form as those Dutch George had found. Since Smith had visited the Santa Rita just two years previously, he obviously considered the two ores to be the same.

It was not until more than two decades later, in the spring of 1854, that anything else was done about the find. By that time Smith had seen the California gold fields and had realized that the discovery made 27 years earlier was in fact a placer gold deposit. Since the placer areas of California were thoroughly staked by then, he decided that it was a good time to return to what was then the northwest corner of New Mexico Territory and mine the untapped deposit. Accordingly, in April, Smith started east from Los Angeles with sixty men to work the placer deposit near the Virgin River.

Somewhere between Los Angeles and their destination, disputes broke out in the party, eventually reducing it to nine men by the time they reached the confluence of the Virgin and Colorado Rivers. For more than a month they searched intensively for the nuggets and found nothing, finally giving up in late May. On June 2, 1854, Smith and his party joined John C. Fremont and traveled with him and his men back to California. At San Bernardino, on June 9, Smith's group split up forever.

Because of his failure to find the gold again, Pegleg Smith's reputation suffered a serious setback, which he was never able to fully overcome. He died in San Francisco in 1866, discredited and penniless. The stories of his successful explorations, though, cannot be diminished. Since he was one of the first to open vast areas of the West, many of the trails he blazed are now paralleled by modern highways. Unfortunately, the site of the juncture of the Virgin and Colorado Rivers is now covered by Lake Mead. Perhaps the nuggets were found somewhere beyond the present lakeshore, or maybe their orgin is now buried under water and silt. With the record he left behind, one does not tend to doubt that Smith's second lost placer deposit does exist somewhere in eastern Clark County.

6. TREASURE OF THE HOWLING CAVE

Somewhere near Paradise Peak, in the Paradise Range of northwestern Nye County, is a strange cave believed to be filled with gold ore and coins. Indians in the area claimed that spirits lived in the cave, although the howling noise probably results from the wind blowing through some natural formation.

In the early days of the central Nevada mining booms, Indians had yet to realize the power of the white man's gold. When they

Rare early photo of Downeyville, taken as a sudden flash flood races down an arroyo in the center of the community.

did acquire some, usually by killing the owners of the gold, they sensed that the yellow metal held much fascination for Caucasians. While the Indians had no use for it, they thought the spirits might like it as a token. Thus they developed the habit of carrying all of the captured gold to the cave and leaving it there for their gods.

One story tells of a gold shipment being sent out from the then-new boom camp of Downeyville. There were only crude milling facilities there yet, so the gold was packed as it came. Flakes, dust, nuggets, and tiny crude bars known as miners' bricks were all placed in heavy sacks and dispatched to Austin. Indians waylaid the shipment, though, killing the guards and making off with anything they could use. When they found the gold they are reported to have carried it to the cave, then dumping it all out on the floor. They might have no use for the gold, but the heavy sacks were perfect for carrying pine nuts.

In the early days of Berlin, a young Indian boy named Jimmy Graham was once taken aside by his mother. Pointing off across Ione Valley in the direction of Paradise Peak, she told the story of the cave. She claimed it went clear through the mountain range and did indeed house captured gold.

Jimmy knew the value of gold quite well, and determined to steal some from the cave. He finally located a squaw who knew where the cave was, but she would not violate the taboo against letting anyone else in on the secret. After much cajoling, he was finally able to bribe her with a sack of flour and a side of bacon. She still would not show him the cave, but she did agree to retrieve some gold for him. As it was well into winter, with a nice blanket of snow on the ground, he gladly let her go alone, confident that he could easily follow her tracks to the cave when she returned.

The squaw did return to Berlin with a small amount of gold, and Jimmy quickly started off on her back trail. Right then a warm storm blew in and it began to rain. In no time the snow was melted, the Indian's tracks disappearing in the mud. He tried everything to convince the squaw to again visit the cave, but she adamantly refused. The Great Spirit, she said, had deliberately obliterated her tracks to keep anyone else from finding the cave.

Another Berlin resident named Ludwick also heard of the cave. He decided to get the gold for himself, but a search of the area only turned up a few old coins. He and a friend then kidnapped a squaw who was thought to know the cave's location. When she decided not to help them, the two men tied her up and suspended her from a tree. They let her hang for awhile, then cut her down. She still refused to give them any assistance, so they hoisted her again. When she was cut down the second time, and still would not help them, they let her go and evidently gave up the search.

One final story concerns Henry LeBeau, a pioneer cattle rancher near Ellsworth. He and an Indian cowboy were chasing cattle in the Paradise Range one day and had ventured into a canyon near Paradise Peak. Suddenly a strange moaning sound came from a clump of cedar trees. In a flash the Indian turned and raced his horse down and out of the canyon. LeBeau was a superstitious man and kept his own horse two jumps behind the Indian's. He later said that he had no idea what caused the sound, but neither he nor the Indian ever ventured near that canyon again.

In all probability, there may well be a howling cave in the Paradise Range. Certainly the Indians of the vicinity still think so, and enough others have been involved in the legend to give it some credence. Whether or not it contains stolen gold, though, will only be determined when someone again locates the mysterious cave.

7. LOST PICKHANDLE MINE

Around the turn of the century a Basque sheepherder was driving a band of sheep from Austin to Indian Valley up the Reese River. He kept to the west side of the valley near the foothills of the Shoshone Mountains as he headed south.

At the mouth of Becker Canyon, near where the trees extended out into the valley, the sheepman discovered a three-inch vein of gold-bearing sugar quartz. As soon as he had dug into the rock to be certain it was an actual vein, he stuck a pick into the crotch of a tree standing off by itself. He placed it so that the pick's handle pointed toward the vein, though he later said that once a person knew where the quartz was, it could be seen from a hundred yards in either direction. The herder left his dogs to watch over the flock and hurried the 45 miles back to Austin to record his claim.

There he found that Becker Canyon was just over the county line in Nye County and he would have to travel 75 miles to Belmont to record his find. The herder returned to his sheep and hurried them south. He sold part of the band in Ione, part in Berlin, and finally disposed of the last head in Grantsville. Free to travel, he lost no time in getting to Belmont, but it was more than a month after he made the discovery that the claim was finally recorded.

With the money from the sale of the sheep, the herder bought supplies for his return to Becker Canyon. But when he got there, he was unable to find any trace of his quartz or of the pick marking it. He searched until his supplies and money ran out, then gave it up and returned to the sheep business.

In 1908, the mining camp of Ursline boomed in Becker Canyon. Extremely high-grade ore was mined, so rich it was called "picture rock," and it all came from white quartz veins no more than three inches wide. All the mines, though, were located in the canyon itself. No vein of white quartz was ever found on the flats below.

Eventually the boom died and the mines closed. The story was almost forgotten until a local prospector heard it and began asking around. He was told of some Indians who some years back had found a pick in a tree in the area of Becker Canyon, but they had traded it for a jug of wine in Austin. He also learned that the Bureau of Land Management had removed the trees on the valley floor, plowed up the topsoil, and planted crested wheat there.

The pick is almost certainly gone; the tree it was in is probably removed; and the vein of white quartz could be covered by wheat. But the gold that the sheepherder found and the Ursline miners missed is likely there yet.

42

8. MORMON WAGON TRAIN TREASURE

In 1856, when outright war loomed imminent between Utah and the federal government, Brigham Young decided to take steps to protect the wealth of the Mormon church. A suitable hiding place was needed and scouts were duly dispatched to locate one. Finally a large cave was found in what is now eastern Nevada between Pioche and Ely.

Meanwhile, every attempt was being made in Utah to convert all possible assets into hard cash. Extra supplies were sold for whatever they would bring to passing travelers, banks were liquidated, and church members were taxed to the fullest. A group of armed guards was stationed at the cave, while the assembled money and bullion was transported in small batches for safekeeping there. The total amount hidden by the church has been estimated at around $1.5 million.

All seemed to be going well until news of the infamous Mountain Meadows Massacre shocked the country. With the burden of this additional unfavorable sentiment, church leaders felt that even the cave was insufficient for the safety of their wealth. Plans were made to ship the entire cache to San Bernardino, from where it could be freighted to Mexico or shipped to some other country. Twenty-two wagons, with an armed escort of forty Utah militiamen, met at the cave and removed all the gold and money. In an attempt to avoid detection the caravan stayed off the existing roads, instead making its way across the then-unmapped deserts of south-central Nevada.

But the desert was too much for even these pioneers to tackle. The wagon train soon found itself critically short of water and unable to locate any in the country it was passing through. The militia finally decided to backtrack to the closest water source to bring up enough for them to continue, leaving the wagons and animals in the care of the teamsters. It took the soldiers several days to secure the water and on their return all that remained were corpses and the charred skeletons of the burned wagons. Paiutes had attacked the small group of teamsters, wiping them out to a man, and there was absolutely no trace of the treasure.

Though they conducted a diligent search, the militia never found any of the wagons' cargo, nor did subsequent searchers sent out by the Mormon church. Later reports of the Paiutes having a secret cache of coins were never verified, and today even the very site of the massacre is a mystery. Recent treasure hunters have settled upon Red Rock Canyon just west of Las Vegas as the possible location of the hidden hoard, but excavations in that area have not produced any of the missing millions. It is known that the Mormon church has not recovered any of the cache, which would be valued by today's collectors at many times the original estimate of $1.5 million.

9 LOST BARKLEY MINE

Charles (Bud) Barkley was born too late to participate in the boom days of the Comstock. But while growing up in Carson City, he heard tale after tale of the mines at Tonopah, Rawhide, and Goldfield. He held down a job as an engineer on the Virginia & Truckee Railroad, but his spare time was often spent hunting or prospecting in the hills.

In 1908, on one of his periodic hunting trips in the mountains west of Washoe Valley, Barkley tripped over a rock hidden in a clump of brush. Angered at his clumsiness, he let loose a kick at the rock, breaking off a chunk in the process. The broken section glittered in the sunlight and Barkley stooped to pick it up. The interior was liberally sprinkled with free gold.

All thoughts of hunting were now gone, and he carefully dug around the small outcrop. Beneath the topsoil he uncovered a vein of gold ore more than three feet wide extending down into the ground. He gathered a small batch of samples, then hurried back to Carson.

His excitement was boundless, until the following day when he attempted to file on the property. The area of his discovery was well within the 42,000 acres owned by the Hobart Estate. As that land had been deeded prior to the 1872 law covering mineral rights, it was impossible to stake a mining claim on it.

Barkley tried to buy the land, but was told that none of it would ever be sold. He then made an open disclosure that he had found gold on the property and asked for a lease to develop it under terms standard at that time. He was told that the estate would pay a nominal fee for showing them where the ore was, but that was all.

This last reply so angered him that Barkley vowed he would never tell them where the gold was hidden. He had carefully covered the deposit to ensure they would never find it unaided. When the assay report came back showing a value of $47,000 to the ton, he chuckled with revenge.

For the next few years Barkley made occasional secret trips to the deposit to take out small batches of ore. Dozens of detectives were hired by the Hobart Estate to follow him to the gold or to attempt to locate it themselves. All failed, so numerous contracts were drawn up in the hopes that he would accept one and show them the deposit. Each document, though, was turned down by Barkley's attorneys, claiming that there was always a clause somewhere that would eventually take their client out of the picture.

Even with the profits he was receiving from the sale of the high-grade, skeptics still claimed Barkley's mine was a fantasy. To quell this rumor, he once took Alexander Ardery, Superintendent of the V.&T. Railroad, to the site. Ardery swore to the unbelievers that the deposit was real, but always kept the secret of the location to himself.

In his 1913 *History of Nevada,* Sam Davis wrote, "Some of the gold exhibited in Carson was so phenomenally rich as to resemble the product of a furnace. Numerous attempts have been made to induce Barkley to disclose the location of the ledge, but without success."

The existence of gold in Little Valley, where the mine is supposed to be located, was verified by W. O. Vanderburg in the University of Nevada Bulletin entitled *Placer Mining in Nevada.* He wrote, "The placer deposits were worked in the early days and the total yield is reported to have been in the neighborhood of $100,000 . . . a value of $60,000 was taken from one pocket."

Barkley never did make peace with the Hobart Estate. He did promise to show his son the deposit as soon as he was discharged from the Navy in World War I, but the father died of pneumonia on December 9, 1918. Superintendent Ardery also took the secret of the mine with him to his grave, and the gold's location was lost.

It remains hidden to this day. As Davis wrote, "One of the richest ledges ever discovered lies in the Sierra mountains but a few miles from Carson City."

10. LOST DEER HUNTER MINE

During the Depression a visiting deer hunter would spend two weeks every fall at the Bowler Ranch on the banks of the Reese River just a few miles south of the Lander County line. He regularly hunted in Barrett Canyon, due west from the Bowler Ranch, and nearly always bagged an animal.

One year the visitor was having a more difficult time finding deer than usual. He had hunted on into the late afternoon hiking high in the canyon up to timberline, where he decided to rest awhile. Leaning his rifle against a tree, the hunter sat on a rock beneath a mountain mahogany to scan the countryside. His glance fell on a piece of pink quartz on the ground near his feet and he bent to retrieve it. The unusual color and its heavy weight prompted the hunter to put it in his pocket and then continue his search for game. At the ranch that night he remembered the rock and showed it to the Bowlers. They commented on its attractive color, so he presented it to them. It was promptly placed on a window sill, where it remained for about ten years.

A prospector visiting them in the 1940's noticed the rock and saw traces of gold showing on the surface. He asked the Bowlers for permission to have it assayed. When they agreed, but asked why he thought it valuable, he promptly broke the rock in half. The center was shot through with gold, and when the assay returns came in it ran $100,000 to the ton!

The hunter who had originally found the specimen heard about the assay results. He immediately quit his job and spent the rest of his life searching Barrett Canyon for the source of the gold.

Few examples of rose quartz occur in the Shoshone Mountains. One batch of barren samples was found in the south fork of the canyon, but none of the myriad prospectors who have hunted for it has ever found more of the gold-bearing pink rock.

11. ELLISON CANYON TREASURE

Twenty-four miles southwest of Ely, near the present junction of State Route 38 and U.S. 6, is Ellison Canyon. In the early 1900's a man named Hayden operated a small money-making ranch at the mouth of the canyon.

Around 1915 the ranch was offered for sale and soon purchased by Owen Cazier for $10,000, part in cattle and part in cash. The new owner wanted to move in as soon as possible, so Hayden immediately started moving to a temporary location. As the old Hamilton-Pioche stage road used to run through Ellison Canyon, he figured that an abandoned station some 11 miles above the ranch might be usable for a short while.

After a few repairs to the old building had been made, Hayden and his Indian housekeeper began hauling their possessions to the new location. One of the last items to be moved was his money cache. Early one morning he dug up the small lard bucket containing his bank. All the money, nearly $17,000, was transferred to two small canvas bags and slung across the pommel of his saddle. He instructed the housekeeper to pack everything but the dishes they would need that night and then he started driving his last twenty head of cattle to the new location higher in the canyon.

That evening, when Hayden had returned to the ranch to spend a last night there, his housekeeper inquired if the savings had been put in a safe place. He told her that no one would ever find it where he had it hidden.

Bright and early next morning he loaded the bed and chairs in the wagon and went to harness the mules while the stove was cooling down enough to be handled. He was gone much longer than necessary, so after the breakfast chores were finished, the Indian went looking for him. She found him face down in the corral, killed by a kick in the head from one of his mules.

Hayden was buried near Ely; his belongings were turned over to the Indian housekeeper and her family. Over the years until her death she searched for the money he had hidden so well, but reportedly never found it and she died penniless. The stone ruins of the old stage station are still visible high in the canyon. Somewhere nearby is $17,000 in gold and silver, still wrapped in the rotting remains of Hayden's two canvas sacks.

12. VIRGINIA CITY BANK LOOT

The morning of October 25, 1927 dawned cool and clear in Virginia City. Bystanders on the boardwalks greeted William J. Henley, manager of the once-booming town's sole remaining bank, as he strode to the corner of C and Taylor Streets to begin the day's business. Some minutes later a green auto careened out from beside the bank, raced down C Street, and turned onto the Six Mile Canyon road. The morning's stillness was shattered further when Henley ran from the old brick building yelling, "The bank's been robbed!"

Within minutes Sheriff T. J. Hurley quickly responded by forming a posse consisting of cars and trucks each loaded with three or four armed citizens. They tore off after the fleeing robbers, while another group of Indian boys mounted on rugged mountain ponies followed in their wake in case the fugitives headed cross country.

Constable Harry Hunter and three armed men were in the posse's lead car. They were the first to reach the bottom of Six

This building, originally the Bank of California, housed the Virginia City Bank in 1927. It was down Taylor Street, to the right of the bank, that Moore and Fitzsimmons' green car sped away with the money.

Mile Canyon where they found the wreck of the green getaway car. They approached cautiously, but quickly realized the auto was abandoned. Nearby tracks indicated the robbers had wrecked the green car deliberately and transferred to another vehicle parked there in readiness. The chase was on again, but now the posse had no idea what type vehicle they were after.

Meanwhile, Pershing County Sheriff J. H. Clawson had been telephoned and was speeding west down Truckee River Canyon. Sparks Chief of Police H. D. Fletcher had also gotten the word and was searching east in the canyon. The two officers met at Clarks Station without either having seen a sign of the outlaws. Together they reasoned that since the Six Mile Canyon road eventually leads to what is now U.S. 50, they would cut across the mountains via the old Ramsey road and try to pick up the trail.

Just three miles south of Clarks Station they spotted a car coming toward them at high speed. The officers pulled over, grabbed their riot shotguns, and waited for the car to approach. When it rounded the last curve in front of them they stepped into the road with the guns at their shoulders. The car skidded to a stop fifty feet away and both men in it raised their hands.

After George Moore and Charlie Fitzsimmons had quietly surrendered, a thorough search of their car was made. Two revolvers and a rifle were found, but the entire amount of money located was only $882.56. By the time the prisoners had been lodged in a Washoe County jail, bank manager Henley had determined that the amount stolen was $32,000.

A mere three hours had elapsed between the time of the holdup and the robbers' capture. With a posse hot on their trail, was there time to bury the money? Or is it possible that more persons were involved and the loot was transferred to them along the way? No one ever knew for certain, and both Moore and Fitzsimmons refused to discuss it. Countless individuals have searched the country between Six Mile Canyon and the old town of Ramsey without ever finding any of the stolen money. If it was buried, then a nice cache of more than $31,000 still lies hidden somewhere along the route.

13 CHIEF NATCHEZ'S LOST MINE

One of the last Nevada Indian chiefs, and son of old Chief Winnemucca, was the Paiute Natchez. For some thirty years he controlled the Indians of western Nevada, leaving almost a dozen sons and daughters when he died. One daughter, Ada, had married Jack Henry, a Shoshone, and was living in the agricultural community of Fernley.

One day in 1919, when she and her husband were talking with the two brothers who were their employers, Ada happened to mention that her father had owned a considerable amount of gold. She claimed he found it in a big canyon farther to the east. When she was a small girl, Natchez had taken her to the canyon and shown her the location of the gold in the event she ever needed to make use of it. This news greatly interested the brothers, but when questioned further about the canyon's location, Ada would only answer that possibly someday she would show it to them.

A year or two passed before Ada spoke further about the gold. Then Jack came to the brothers one day and told them that she was ready to lead them to the site of the deposit in return for the kindness they had shown to her and her husband. They quickly packed enough supplies for a four day trip and took the road from Fernley to Fallon, thirty miles east. From there they headed northeast along the edge of the Stillwater Range until they reached the White Cloud Mountains, where Ada said they would find a canyon marked by strange rocks which looked as if they had been heaped in a pile.

As they were driving near the mountains, she pointed to a canyon and stated that it was the one containing the gold. As they reached the mouth, Ada seemed puzzled by the lack of the distinctive rock formation, although she still felt they had come to the right place.

In camp that night at the canyon's mouth, Ada also told how she was certain she could find the gold again as Natchez had left a marker for her when he brought her there years earlier. Some distance from the deposit itself he had taken off his buckskin jacket and tied it securely to a bush, then showed her exactly how to turn from it to find the gold.

The next morning they started up the canyon on foot, and about noon Ada said they were nearing the spot. They spread out and had slowly begun a systematic search of the canyon, when Jack cried out that he had found an old piece of buckskin tied to the bottom of a bush. This was identified as Natchez's marker, but either the directions had slipped her mind or the sight of the jacket had given her a change of heart. Ada stated that she could lead them no farther.

The men spent the rest of the day searching the area and found nothing. They even tried panning at the mouth of the canyon, getting a few colors for their work, but the dirt generally turned up barren. After two days of looking and finding no trace of the gold, they gave up and returned to Fernley.

For some years afterward the two brothers made periodic trips back to the canyon, but they always returned empty handed. They never doubted the validity of the story, as Natchez was remembered to have jewelry and bracelets fashioned from pure gold. It must have come from somewhere in the Paiute territory. With Ada's story for verification, there is a good chance that the riches still lie somewhere near that remote canyon in the White Cloud Mountains.

14. TYBO'S CHARCOAL KILNS TREASURE

In the mid-1870's, with mining active all over Nevada, charcoal was in great demand for operating the lead-silver smelters. In the Tybo district, where three beehive charcoal ovens were built near the top of McCann's Summit, a number of wood contractors made charcoal from pinyon trees and supplied it to the local mills.

One certain Portuguese contractor was owed a large sum of money by a Tybo smelter. On the day he collected it he decided to go the twenty-odd miles into Tybo to hire more woodcutters. First, as he always did, he cached a portion of the money in a hiding place. It was known that he was saving all that he could to purchase passage for the rest of his family to come to the United States and help him in his business.

After the routine chore of safeguarding his money, the contractor started for Tybo. A short while later he was found where his horse had thrown him. A broken neck had caused his instantaneous death.

Later, one of the contractor's laborers recalled that whenever his employer went to cache money he walked northwest from the dugout located across the road from the charcoal ovens. He also must have gone some distance as the trees near the ovens had all been cut by that time. Probably his homemade bank was over a ridge and out of sight, as the laborer said he was usually gone about three quarters of an hour.

Upper Tybo in 1875. The road to Belmont via McCann's Summit curves left behind the hill in the center background.

53

Although a number of individuals have searched for this treasure, estimated at $4,000 to $6,000, no one has ever reported finding it. Tybo's mines and mills closed in 1891 but did reopen for intermittent operations up to the present time. Tybo itself is a ghost town, with its remaining buildings empty. The trio of ovens still stand on McCann's Summit, landmarks to the cache of a man who buried his dreams in gold coin.

15 LOST PADRE MINE

Although Spanish exploration into modern northwestern Nevada has never been proven, a legend persists of a gold discovery made by an 18th century Spanish expedition. This find was supposedly documented in elaborate detail in the records of the priest leading the expedition, and was filed away in the church archives in Mexico City.

It was not until the latter part of the 19th century that a Mexican researcher happened upon these records and realized that the gold they found might still be there. He called upon an American friend to aid him in locating the deposit, and together they formed a party to go back into the area north of Pyramid Lake to search for it. These records were extremely detailed, including the latitude and longitude of the find, with a map drawn by the priest more than a century earlier. The searchers had no doubt that the gold could be easily located with these directions, and they confidently headed north.

One of the first landmarks on the map was a certain boiling spring, located near modern Gerlach. Here the gold seekers camped for a few days, elated by the fact that the latitude and longitude exactly matched that of the priest's records.

From the spring the map pointed the way north along what had become the Honey Lake road, then the searchers had to travel northeast without the aid of even a trail. They traveled as far as the Pueblo Mountains, just short of High Rock Canyon, and finally camped on the edge of these mountains right where the map said the gold was.

With eager anticipation the party split into small groups and began systematically covering the area. Soon, though, their anticipation turned to disappointment. No trace of the gold could be found. They spent weeks searching the area, eventually heading south with only two tiny placer nuggets. The long hoped-for gold deposit was never located.

Perhaps the gold is still there; perhaps an early-day prospector cleaned it out and covered over his tracks; or maybe there was no gold at all. Until the day that another researcher can make public the Spanish records, the lost Padre remains just another Nevada legend.

16 POST HOLE GOLD

In the early 1920's, the three major ranchers in the Reese River Valley decided to build a drift fence along the Shoshone Mountains to keep their cattle from mingling. The O'Toole Ranch owned grazing rights in Ione Valley while the Bell and Keogh Ranches grazed the Reese, and the fence would greatly simplify roundups. An Italian laborer was hired to begin the fence up from Brush Rabbit Spring on the Reese River side to eventually cross over and down Milton Canyon on the Ione side. Soon after beginning, a strange rock appeared in a post hole he was digging. Upon close examination, the rock turned out to be rose quartz shot through with gold.

The laborer headed into Austin and soon news of the find led to the founding of a tent camp at nearby Woodchuck Spring. Prospect holes were dug all over the area, but not another piece of rose quartz was ever found. On top of that, the discoverer refused to return to look for any more gold. After the excitement died he was asked why, and he replied that he did not want to get gold fever and spend the rest of his life looking for it.

Perhaps there is a gold deposit hidden near Brush Rabbit Spring, and perhaps not. Rose quartz is very rare in that area; not a single color has ever been panned there; and Milton Canyon was once a common route for prospectors heading from Ione Valley to Austin in the late 19th century. An ore specimen could easily have fallen by the wayside and rested there until found by the fence builder. On the other hand, gold is where you find it, and there could be a bonanza of gold-bearing rose quartz somewhere nearby.

An early-day Indian encampment, such as might have been found at Deep Hole in northern Washoe County.

17. LOST INDIAN MINE

Sometime in the 1870's, when settlements in northern Nevada were few and far between, a pioneer named Job Taylor opened a trading post just over the California state line in Indian Valley. Since this store was the only one for miles around, for years he was able to sell supplies to many residents of northwestern Nevada, Indians and whites alike.

Money was nearly as scarce as stores in those days, so the customers in Taylor's often paid for their purchases with furs, other goods, and sometimes gold specimens. Even so, he was quite surprised one day when a young Indian came shopping and paid for his supplies with gold nuggets "as large as hen's eggs." When questioned about the source of his wealth, the Indian hurriedly gathered his purchases and left, giving no answer whatsoever to Taylor's inquiries.

More than a year later the Indian returned for more supplies. Again the trader questioned him about the gold. Just as before, the Paiute paid for the goods with nuggets, said not one word about their origin, and hurried away as soon as he could.

Once again, the following year, the Indian returned to the store, but this time changing tactics Taylor began winning the man's confidence. Eventually, in return for a certain amount of supplies from the trading post, the Paiute agreed to show him to the spot where he gathered the gold. Elated over this turn of events, Taylor contacted Captain Wetherell, a veteran Indian fighter, and the three men started east into Nevada. As the Paiute described it, their destination was a mountain stream, lined in places with trees and filled with gold nuggets as well as trout.

After passing through Susanville, the three-man party stayed on the old Honey Lake road and finally made camp one night at Deep Hole Spring, eight miles northwest of present Gerlach. At the same time Old Winnemucca, chief of the Paiutes, was holding council on Granite Mountain adjacent to Deep Hole. Taylor's Indian guide, who was also carrying a message from his people in California to the Paiutes in Nevada, took an extra day to meet with the old chief. When he returned to the camp at Deep Hole he apologized, but stated that Winnemucca had been very angry when he found out where the Indian was leading the two whites and absolutely forbade him to continue. He even went so far as to promise certain death if they did not immediately turn back to California. Under these conditions there was no alternative but to retrace their steps to Indian Valley.

Whether Winnemucca frightened him or whether he simply had no gold to trade, the Indian never returned to the store. But the following summer a Paiute boy came to buy supplies and made

57

his purchases with similar nuggets. Taylor quickly made friends with the boy and had no trouble getting him to talk. While the boy knew all about the gold-filled stream, he had never actually seen it. He said he did know an old exiled Indian living near Deep Hole who might be induced to guide them to it.

Again Taylor and Wetherell, with the boy, journeyed east until they reached Deep Hole. There they found the old Paiute, but while considered an outcast he was still loyal to the tribe. He refused to lead the whites to the gold under any conditions whatsoever.

This time, though, the two men refused to give up. They demanded that the boy lead them as close as possible to where his elders gathered their nuggets. Frightened, but with no other choice, he claimed it was only "two sleeps" east of Deep Hole, and they continued on.

After two days of traveling the three made camp. According to the young Indian they were still quite a distance from the area of the stream. That night, as Taylor and Wetherell lay in their blankets, they discussed the prospects of finding the gold. Believing that the boy was asleep, Wetherell said that the little Indian had better be true to his word if he knew what was good for him. The tone of voice frightened the boy more than anything else did and, when dawn broke, he slipped away and soon was long gone.

The two men continued to search for a while but eventually they turned back without success. Many times thereafter Taylor traveled the country "two sleeps" beyond Deep Hole, searching canyon after canyon for the right stream. Eventually he felt that the nugget-filled canyon was the one located just south of Virgin Valley.

Legend has it that this canyon had been worked by Indians before the area was ever settled by white men. Another legend infers that the canyon is in reality the site of the lost Blue Bucket gold of Oregon fame. Be that as it may, the canyon hides whatever secret it may possess, for the walls are so steep that masses of rock have fallen and choked the narrow gorge. The canyon is now nearly impassible except on foot, and if gold is there it will be a long time before it will be found.

18. GENOA NAIL KEG CACHE

Late in the spring of 1860, while the rush to "Washoe" was in full swing, the main road from Hangtown (Placerville) over the Sierra to Virginia City was continually packed with miners, prospectors, businessmen, teamsters, all headed for the new diggings on Sun Mountain. This road came off the mountains into Carson Valley at a small community originally called Mormon Station but now known as Genoa.

A view looking north, up Genoa's main street, as it appeared in 1870.

Since there was a shortage of coinage in the new mining area, it was difficult to meet payrolls. Most of the money used to pay the miners had to be shipped in from California by stage. Because of the large number of treasure shipments, stage robberies became a fairly common occurrence, many of these payrolls never reaching their destination.

One shipper thought to outwit robbers by hiding his coin shipment in a nail keg and sending it as simple freight. But someone found out about the plan, and a few miles out of Genoa the coach was stopped. Nothing was taken but the keg, which was rolled off into the woods by two masked highwaymen.

A search was immediately organized, but no trace of the stolen gold or of the men who took it was ever uncovered. The excitement soon died away, and the story was almost forgotten until a miner lay dying in a Montana boom camp. Before he passed away, he said that he wanted to make a confession. He stated that he and another man had pulled the coach robbery back in 1860. They had taken a keg filled with gold coins only a short distance from the road and opened it. Inside was $20,000 in twenty-dollar gold pieces, of which the men took $1,000 apiece, burying the remainder beneath a tall pine which stood nearby. Soon afterwards the pair left the country and never returned.

When the old-timer's story reached Carson Valley, treasure fever broke out in a rash. Many of the trees near Genoa were dug around, and the area near the old stage road was searched thoroughly, but with no success. Then in 1882 a huge avalanche hit, destroying a part of Genoa, carrying away countless trees on the surrounding slopes.

The gold may or may not have been affected by the slide, but numerous discoveries of coins through the years have kept the story alive. In 1916 a blacksmith and his son, while digging around trees in search of the treasure, discovered a chest containing $2,000. In 1948 a cache of undetermined value was found while excavating for a basement. Finally, in 1961, about a hundred $20 gold pieces were found in a nearby hillside. All this has spurred on the search, but the $18,000 in a now rotten nail keg may yet await a lucky finder—if it will ever be found at all.

19. PRICE'S LOST GOLD MINE

In the foothills below Slide Mountain, just above Bowers Mansion in Washoe Valley, nestles one of the most beautiful spots in the Sierra, Price's Lake. Only a short hike from U.S. 395, this lake hides a goodly number of pan-frying trout as well as one of Nevada's most little-known lost mine legends, the story of William Price and his fabulous nuggets.

For many years during the Comstock boom days, Price spent his days alone in the mountains on quiet prospecting trips. Legend maintains that every so often he would appear at Bowers Landing on the Virginia & Truckee Railroad and catch a train to Carson City. Every time he did so he would be carrying a small sack of gold nuggets. He would exchange them for gold coin at the U.S. Mint in Carson, purchase a few supplies, and again disappear into the hills.

People naturally wondered where the gold was coming from; a number of the most curious often tried to follow him. On every trip, though, he managed to lose them before they got any inkling of the location of his wealth. After awhile Price seemed to spend

more time in the vicinity of the lake and people automatically began calling it Price's Lake. Eventually they associated it with the area in which the gold must be located, but try as they would, no one could ever follow him to it.

The years passed and Price grew quite elderly. Finally he decided he had worked enough in mining for gold and decided to retire. He said later that he covered up all traces of his mine, took all his accumulated gold, and caught his last train near Bowers. He never came back.

Although the search for his gold mine has been going on ever since, no one has ever been known to find it. The gold must still be there, but snows and rains of many years have by now obliterated any evidence of the mine's entrance. The ground is very unstable on Slide Mountain, hence its name, and the mine may now be covered with a thick layer of earth. But whatever the present circumstance, Price should be remembered as one Nevada prospector who really did "make good," and still managed to live to enjoy it.

20. SNOWSHOE THOMPSON'S LOST MINE

In the days before the railroads came west, when all transportation between California and Nevada was expensive, slow, and very uncertain, mail delivery was a persistent problem. One of the communities thus affected was Genoa, originally called Mormon Station. The first settlement in Nevada, it soon gained importance as a supplier of agricultural products grown in Carson Valley. Genoa was also a way-station for freighters and travelers passing between California and the Washoe silver region and thus it needed the communication which only the mail could provide.

In summer this road was traveled with little difficulty. But in the winter months, when the high passes were choked with snow, the mail was halted. A solution seemed impossible and those affected felt all that could be done was to wait for progress to improve conditions.

However, an answer was found in John A. Thompson. This tall Norwegian offered to carry mail from Placerville to Genoa and back in the dead of winter, but he was scoffed at until he proved it could be done. Time after time he skied alone over the Sierras, often in bad weather, with a pack of mail strapped to his back. The stories of his feats spread throughout the West and "Snowshoe" Thompson, nicknamed for his long wooden snowshoes or skis, became a legend in his own time.

On one of his periodic trips from west to east, he crossed the last summit and paused to enjoy the view stretching out across Nevada. Some years before he had moved his family into a small house in Diamond Valley, south of Genoa, and as he rested he could look directly down at his home. As he got to his feet, a glance at an outcrop of quartz stopped him, for the white rock was streaked with gold. He gathered a few samples and finished the trip, saying nothing about his find to anyone but his wife.

John A. "Snowshoe" Thompson, who carried the mail over the Sierras between Genoa and Placerville from 1856 until just before his death in 1876. A contemporary historian wrote, "he courted, rather than feared, the perils of the mountains."

Thompson had a job to do and it was more important than wealth. On later trips he brought back more ore samples and sometimes talked with his wife of the gold he had found and how they would not have to worry about money when he eventually retired. In his mind he planned how to develop the property, where to build the road to it, and numerous other details that would be necessary when the time came to take out the gold. That day never arrived though, for while plowing and seeding one spring he came down with pneumonia. On May 15, 1876, "Snowshoe" Thompson died.

He left no map to his gold outcrop and had never even taken a member of his family to see it. Some laughed at the idea of his ever having found gold, but others remembered his passion for truthfulness, and the ore samples in his home left no doubt that Thompson had indeed found gold in the nearby mountains.

His wife and son, practically penniless, moved away, but left behind one clue to the location of the quartz outcrop. They remembered how Thompson through the years had remarked that from his house in the valley he could look up and see directly where the gold was. In the decades since then many people have stood in that valley and also looked up, searching for a lead to the quartz. The ground between Horseshoe Canyon and Hawkins' Peak has been combed by prospectors time and again, but never with success. Those who know the legend, and the facts behind it, have no doubt that "Snowshoe" Thompson's lost mine is a reality. To this day it still lies somewhere in the high Sierras above the Diamond Valley home of a great Nevada pioneer.

21. THREE POOLS OF GOLD

In 1844, a military scouting party consisting of Captain Applegate, Captain Scott, and a guide named Garrison, set out to break a new trail across northwestern Nevada. They left the main emigrant trail at Lassen's Meadow, north of the present town of Lovelock, and crossed the barren Black Rock Desert northwesterly toward Oregon.

Near a group of lakes, known today as Massacre, Middle, and West Lakes, Paiute Indians attacked the explorers. They fought well, but before the Indians could be driven off, Scott was wounded and Garrison killed. From that engagement until the Paiute's final defeat at Pyramid Lake in 1860, this new trail, known as the Applegate-Lassen Cut-Off in honor of Captain Applegate and California pioneer Peter Lassen, was always subject to attack.

In 1851, a small emigrant party left the Humboldt River and started along this trail to Oregon. Less than a year earlier a much larger train had been attacked at Massacre Lake, giving it its name. They had forty dead before the battle was finished, but the owners of the five emigrant wagons felt they could get through. After leaving the river they managed to cross the Black Rock Desert and safely reach Emigrant Spring, in what is now northern Washoe County.

That night, after the stock were bedded and the men and women settled into their regular camp routine, a light rain began to fall. It kept up all night but stopped just before dawn. At daylight the storm was gone, and so were all the emigrants' animals. By using the rain as cover, Indians had crept in and taken the herd, leaving the travelers in a desperate situation.

As soon as the loss was discovered, the men in the party armed themselves and set off following the tracks of the rustled stock. Having walked for hours with no success, by noon some of the men felt obliged to return to the wagons for the safety of the women and children. Three agreed to continue on to try to find the animals.

Late in the afternoon the three trackers found themselves in a narrow canyon full of good grass and a clear flowing stream. At the head of the canyon the stream had formed a small waterfall with three crystal-clear pools at its base. While kneeling to drink from one of these pools, the emigrants found gold nuggets scattered along its bottom.

One man had a tin cup on his belt which he began filling with the yellow nuggets. Not until it was full did he realize that the cup would be awkward to carry back, so he buried it in a shallow hole at the base of a dead pine. Then, as the three men filled pockets and bandannas with gold and were scrambling about the stream searching for more, Indians opened fire from the canyon-top. Two of the emigrant fell dead but the third, Stoddard, raced out of the canyon as quickly as possible.

By hiding in the brush and rocks, Stoddard eventually managed to elude the Indians, but in so doing he also lost his way. He did not know how to return to the wagons except by backtracking, which he felt certain would only ensure his capture or death. From a hilltop he sighted a tall, densly-wooded mountain in the far distance and started walking toward it. Once off the high ground, though, he quickly became lost again, wandering aimlessly among the sage-covered hills.

Many days later, ragged and almost dead, Stoddard stumbled into Downieville, California. Practically insane from his ordeal, he babbled deliriously of Indians, gold, and of his endless walking. He was given the best care possible and eventually recovered enough to tell his story in detail, relating the entire experience to anyone who would listen.

One man who heard Stoddard tell his tale was Major Downie. Often in his later life he told of when that half-dead man, clutching a bandanna full of gold nuggets, stumbled into town. Others also heard the story and saw the gold, and many of them traveled into Nevada to look for the gold. None ever found it.

Changes of terrain are frequent up in that High Rock country. Snow, flash floods, earthquakes, and the wind all destroy and rebuild the topography. Because of this, the narrow canyon and the gold-filled stream may be gone. Whatever the case, the gold was there, but that rugged country even today keeps tight rein on its secrets and seldom lets them slip out.

McCann's Station at the summit of the Tybo-Belmont road, taken after the station had been abandoned. Men in photo are campers.

22. McCANN'S SUMMIT GAMBLER'S CACHE

In the 1870's and 1880's, Tybo was one of Nevada's more important mining communities. The population was nearing 1,000 residents with numerous businesses supplying every need. The town boasted such refinements as a brick school, a literary society, a newspaper, Good Templar's lodge, and a post office. But the most important, as usual, were the saloons and gambling halls. On paydays they were definitely the hub of the town.

One particular payday a gambler from Belmont, then the seat of Nye County, came to town to relieve the miners of their wages. Within two nights he had hit a fabulous run of luck, winning more than $3,000. The third day, though, he decided it was time to leave before someone took offense at his winnings. He had already heard whispers that a number of those who had lost heavily in his games were beginning to talk of forcefully regaining their money.

The gambler boarded the stage at the edge of town and headed back toward Belmont with his winnings contained in a canvas ore sack. The driver later described him as being armed, nervous, and looking as though he expected to be ambushed any moment.

At McCann's Summit, a few miles west of Tybo at the head of the canyon, the driver usually stopped for a few minutes to let the horses blow. Here the gambler handed a $5 gold piece to the driver and asked him to wait at the charcoal kilns about a mile down the road. He then took his sack of money and disappeared into the trees.

The driver did as he had been asked and halted at the kilns. He later stated that the gambler couldn't have hidden his sack very far from the road as the stage had only been waiting some ten minutes when he showed up empty-handed. He again boarded the coach for Belmont, telling the driver he would return for his canvas sack after the Tybo people had cooled off a bit. He was never able to make that return trip though, as within the week a poor loser at a Belmont poker table ended the gambler's life with a well-placed shot from a cap and ball derringer.

It wasn't too long before Tybo began to decline. The story of the gambler's cache was almost forgotten so there is a chance that it was never located. It may still lie today in a shallow, hand-dug hole somewhere along that mile between McCann's Summit and the kilns.

23. TIM CODY'S LOST LEDGE

In 1908, after the great strikes of Tonopah, Goldfield, and Rawhide had drawn tens of thousands of people into the Nevada deserts, prospectors continued their search for bigger and better finds. Tim Cody was one such prospector and was that year camped at Stewart Springs some 15 miles from Goldyke. Using the springs as base, he systematically covered all of the surrounding country for signs of ore.

Eventually his supplies began to run low, so he decided to travel to Goldyke to obtain more. On that day, an overcast winter morning, he set out on foot for the store 15 miles away. It was just his bad luck that the overcast blew up into a storm and Cody was soon lost.

He located an abandoned mine tunnel and spent the night there somewhat protected from the storm. The following morning, with a clear sky marking the end of the bad weather, he started to climb a ridge nearby to get his bearings. Part way up he happened to stumble upon a rich gold vein in a quartz outcrop. Cody picked up a few ore samples and continued up the ridge. From the top, as he later stated, he could clearly see Paradise Peak as well as Rawhide Peak to the northwest. But even knowing the landmarks did not seem to help and he soon became lost again, reaching Goldyke after much difficulty.

Once resupplied, Cody tried time and time again to find the gold-laden quartz and always failed. Eventually after he gave it up and moved on, the story became just another half-believed Nevada legend. Then in 1949, three men appeared in the area searching for the lost ledge. Evidentally Cody had told someone about it who believed him, for the three men also had a map drawn by the prospector to guide them.

But Cody couldn't find the gold and his map wasn't able to lead anyone to it. Somewhere in the hills south of Gabbs the ledge is still there. Judging from all the fruitless searching of the past decades, it may take someone getting lost again to find it.

*Typical Nevada prospector's outfit, photo-
graphed around the turn of the century. It may
have been a prospector using such a rig as this
who discovered the now lost blue vein
containing diamonds.*

24. LOST DIAMOND MINE

From the discovery of the great Comstock Lode in 1859 to the last Nevada mineral rush in 1928, numerous prospectors have been combing every hill and canyon for signs of gold and silver ore. Thousands of strikes have been made, a few worth millions and many worthless, but in most cases the ores were gold, silver and copper. A few people realized what variety of metals there was in Nevada though, and some strikes were made in lead, manganese, nickel, and marble. There was even a platinum mine—but no one ever expected to find diamonds.

In 1872, as the story goes, one of Nevada's drifting prospectors headed into the southernmost part of Lincoln (now Clark) County to see what he could find. After spending the night at the Gass Ranch, just north of present downtown Las Vegas, he started due south into the McCullough Mountains. The prospector had covered about 30 miles when he ran across a streak of blue clay in a volcanic formation. Thinking there might be something in the deposit, he took samples and panned them. When all that showed up were a few crystals, he continued on his way.

Quite some time later the prospector happened to show the crystals to a jeweler who informed him they were actually diamonds. Jubilant over this unusual find, the prospector gave most of the stones away to friends, confident that he could always return and work his claim. When he traveled back into the McCullough's though, he never could locate the blue clay again. He searched and searched, but at the time of the discovery he had thought the clay to be worthless. He had not marked its location in his mind, and he never saw it again.

PROSPECTERS OUTFIT   GOLD FIELD NEVADA & MANHATTAN

The story was often told in the mining camps of southern Nevada, but as diamonds had never before been found within the state, there were very few people who believed the tale. Then in July 1905, E. L. Hews located a diamond mine three and a half miles southeast of Tonopah. All of a sudden Nevada experienced a "diamond rush" with hundreds of people flocking to the claims situated on the Tonopah-Silver Bow road. But the excitement was short-lived and the boom died when experts concluded that the diamonds were of poor grade and practically worthless.

With the existence of diamonds in Nevada an accepted fact, the old story of the lost diamond mine in Clark County is now looked upon more favorably. There indeed may be a vein of diamonds in the McCullough Mountains, but it is also possible that, as in the rush of 1905, the stones may be completely worthless. On the other hand, no one knows what treasures might lie beneath the surface of that thin streak of blue clay.

Bridge Street looking north, Winnemucca, c. early 1870's.

25. WINNEMUCCA STAGECOACH TREASURE

In many cases throughout the Far West, where "civilization" had not yet arrived, certain forms of outlawry were actually condoned. Stage and train robbers were often regarded as folk heroes, because of a universal dislike of freight company rates. The public at that time considered their escapades a matter of thieves robbing thieves.

Unfortunately for the outlaws the law seldom thought that way. Often highwaymen were so dogged by a determined deputy or undersheriff that they simply stopped running and gave up. On more than one occasion the loot from a robbery was buried during the flight and the money never recovered because the robbers were either killed or imprisoned.

This was the case in the late 1860's when the Winnemucca-Boise stage was held up just outside of Winnemucca. The robbery occurred at the north end of the bridge crossing the Humboldt River at Bridge Street. Two carefully masked men stopped the coach and removed the mail pouch and three large bars of bullion. The coach immediately hurried into town and the driver notified the law. J. N. Thacker, the county Sheriff, was in pursuit within minutes after the holdup.

74

The two masked men had left the area with such speed that Thacker knew they could not possibly have carried the three heavy ingots with them. He never did capture the outlaws, but he always believed that the loot from the stage was hidden near the bridge, probably in the riverbank. For months after the robbery the river near Bridge Street was guarded night and day while an intensive search was conducted, but nothing was ever found. Eventually, as with all such occurrences, the excitement died and the incident was forgotten.

Thacker's reputation and determination in the field of law enforcement continued to grow; by the turn of the century he was Chief Detective for Wells Fargo. Thus he was not surprised when, in 1904, Shirley Browning and George Sanford found the rotting mail bag which had been stolen in the robbery forty years earlier. To bear up Thacker's theory, the bag was discovered in the mud of the riverbank very close to Bridge Street.

People in the area maintain that the three bars of bullion are still along the riverbank somewhere, as it is certain that the robbers had no chance of riding off with them. It must also be concluded that they are hidden quite well, as the weight of the bars and the yearly high water of the Humboldt would make them sink ever deeper into the sand and mud. Three large bars of gold bullion though, in any riverbank, is certainly a treasure worth digging for.

A 1910 view of Winnemucca's Bridge Street bridge spanning the Humboldt River.

26. LOST MONTE CRISTO MINE

In the latter part of the 1890's, Nevada's economy was depressed. A number of the state's mines had either cut back drastically or closed down. This put scores of men out of work, men who knew nothing but mining, and many departed for Arizona and Colorado. The only thing left for those who stayed behind was to go prospecting. Coupled with the amount of men who were constantly prospecting anyway, this meant that a very large number of fortune seekers were combing the back country of Nevada.

In 1896, one of these itinerant gold seekers, John Lampson of Pahranagat Valley, was passing through the Monte Cristo Mountains in Esmeralda County, prospecting as he went along. Near Crow Spring, on a twin-topped reddish hill, he found extremely high-grade float and staked a claim. Though he thoroughly searched the countryside, he never could locate the vein from which it had come. Finally giving up in disgust, he gave his ore samples and the story of his find to his best friend, John Gilbert.

Gilbert realized the value of the ore, as Lampson had, and determined to try to find it. With another prospector named Thompson accompanying him, Gilbert headed into the Monte Cristos and quickly found the area Lampson had described to him. At first his efforts proved futile, with the two men finding nothing more than ore running $7 a ton, but while hunting in ever larger circles from their camp, he found a rich lead-silver deposit which became known as the Carrie mine.

In 1897, Gilbert moved his family to the Carrie and began working it in earnest to make a paying mine out of it. With the founding of Tonopah in 1900 and the subsequent rush there, Gilbert and his family sold out, moved to the new town, and quite forgot about the originally searched-for deposit in the Monte Cristos.

Then one day in 1919, Lampson showed up in Tonopah and ran into Gilbert. After some talk and a bit of persuasion, Lampson agreed to show him where he had found the ore back in 1896. Together the two men started into the Monte Cristos, but Lampson led them to a location quite distant from the area he had originally described to Gilbert. When questioned about that, Lampson claimed he could prove it was the original site because he had left two claim markers in the vicinity. After a brief search a marker was found nearby and the date on it read "June 6, 1896."

Gilbert again started a search of the area as Lampson had done 23 years earlier, and again found nothing. But the Monte Cristos held some sort of attraction for him, and he kept returning to prospect them year after year. His work finally paid off in 1924, when he located a strike which quickly grew into the mining boom town of Gilbert.

The story of a hidden ore body near Crow Spring had prompted many men to prospect the area, but nothing of consequence was ever found. Lampson never again hunted for the ore after he told Gilbert about it and the latter, after making two rich strikes in the Monte Cristos, also quit searching for it.

The Gilbert mines eventually played out and the town was abandoned in the early 1930's, thus finally emptying the Monte Cristo Mountains of inhabitants. But within a mile of Crow Spring, on a small reddish hill with twin tops, there still should be the remains of two claim markers, the only tangible clues that might point to the location of the phantom Monte Cristo mine.

77

27. SAND DUNE WHISKEY CACHE

When someone speaks or writes about hidden treasure, it is invariably gold, silver, or some precious commodity. This century-old "treasure," however, is nothing as common as silver ingots or gold double eagles, but an entire wagon load of whiskey, a product nearly as desirable in its day as the money used to buy it.

In the 1880's, an independent freighter contracted to carry a load of casks of 100-proof whiskey from northern California to the mining camps of northern Arizona. His departure point and route are unknown, but he did stop over a few days at a ranch in Oasis Valley. Continuing south, the freighter was forced to halt when a powerful storm caught him near the sand dune 23 miles south of Beatty, in southern Nye County. Wind-whipped sand made further progress impossible, so he hobbled his animals and took refuge under the wagon.

The storm raged all day and through the night. It was not until the following dawn that the skies cleared, the wind died, and the freighter prepared to resume his journey. But though he searched in all directions, his horses had vanished, and the drifting sand had obscured any tracks.

Typical of a 19th century freight wagon, a vehicle such as this may still be buried under a sand dune in southern Nye County.

Taking all the water he could carry, the teamster made the walk back to Oasis Valley in a day and a half. There he explained his dilemma and borrowed a hitch of draft horses to use in recovering his outfit. He drove them back to the area of the sand dune, but this time not a trace could be found of his wagon! There were no tracks of any sort, and the freighter concluded that another storm must have shifted a portion of the huge dune, completely covering his wagon and its cargo. He gave up the search as hopeless, returned the horses to Oasis Valley, and went his way.

As Oasis Valley is about 100 miles northwest of the sand dune over rough mountains and valleys, the teamster could never have walked there in a day and a half. Moreover, in the 1880's freight from northern California sent to the northern Arizona mining camps was routed through central California, and shipped by rail to Needles and Kingman on the Santa Fe Railroad. So this version of the sand dune whiskey tale contains historical inaccuracies.

A version accepted by the residents of the area places the date early in this century and the site of the stop-over as Rose's Well, a then active stage station about 18 miles south of Beatty. Stanley W. Paher concisely relates this tale in his *Nevada Ghost Towns and Mining Camps*, claiming that the teamster left Rose's Well after a short stop in 1910. When the big storm hit him at the sand dune, he cut the horses loose. Abandoning the wagon, the teamster took his animals back to Rose's Well to wait out the storm. When the skies finally cleared, the teamster brought the horses back to the dune to pick up the wagon and resume his trip, but was unable to find any trace of his vehicle or its cargo.

Regardless of the version of the story, the wagon has yet to be found. The discovery of a heavy freight wagon laden with casks of whiskey would be a sensational story. The desert tends to preserve what it captures, so the whiskey may well be mellowed to an unprecedented character. But whatever might be its flavor after all these years, this cache ranks among Nevada's most unusual "treasures."

28. SWEDE PETE'S LOST MINE

Late one year, sometime in the early 1900's, an itinerant handyman known as Swede Pete worked as a cowhand on the Cold Creek Ranch in White Pine County. The fall roundup had just been completed and the ranch was laying off hands in anticipation of the coming winter. Then, while making a check of the range, one of the riders ran across a small herd that had been missed during roundup. Someone had to take the cattle to the shipping yards at Elko, and Pete was chosen for the task. His instructions were to put them on the railroad before the first snow. As soon as they were gathered he started north.

His route from Cold Creek to Elko was an easy, well used one, heading up Newark Valley and along Huntington Creek much the same as State Route 228 does today. But the cattle were spooky from being driven so hard, keeping Pete busy pushing strays who tried to break away back into the herd.

As they were traveling along the east edge of Huntington Creek, between Overland Pass and Jiggs, three young steers bolted from the herd and headed east toward the timber. Pete took a moment to push the herd farther onto the flat, then turned after the strays. Two of the steers were immediately caught and returned to the herd. Pete then set out on the tracks of the third, though by this time the steer had a good start and had disappeared into the trees.

With his eyes on the tracks, Pete noticed where the steer had crossed a low outcrop of gray quartz. He stopped and looked at the rock, then stepped down and examined it more carefully. The quartz was shot full of free gold! He quickly put some of the ore into his saddlebags and kicked enough dirt over the outcrop to hide it. To indicate the site he piled rocks near the ledge and placed a long jagged piece of pink rock on top which pointed directly to the gold. As an additional marker, he took his small prospector's pick and drove it into a nearby ceder with the blunt end pointing toward the vein.

Pete mounted again and hurried after the stray, which he soon caught and returned to the herd. He gathered the cattle and pushed them north even faster than before.

At the town of Jiggs, Pete couldn't contain himself any longer and decided to put the cattle into a pen for the night so he could celebrate the find of his new wealth. In a local saloon he showed everyone samples and told his story repeatedly while downing many shots of whiskey. For hours the boys in the saloon tried their best to find out the location of the rich ore, but all Pete would tell them was how he had placed his markers above the vein located on a small cedar-covered knoll.

In the early morning hours he said goodnight to his many new friends and stumbled out into the night. After dawn some cowboys found him in an irrigation ditch where he had fallen, too drunk to get up. They took him to a nearby house where he was put to bed and nursed as well as possible, but pneumonia set in and Swede Pete eventually died.

The tale he told that night in the Jiggs saloon became a legend in the area, and an extensive search was begun for his two monuments, though without success. Pete's markers may probably be there yet, though the pick head will be much deeper in the cedar due to its growth in the intervening years. Most important though, is that the gold has never been found again. All a searcher needs to do to become wealthy is to choose the right cedar-covered hill from the dozens along the west side of the Ruby Mountains.

29. IONE'S BURIED BULLION

Soon after the turn of the century, the Nevada Stokes Company instituted an innovative measure to protect its payroll on the trip from Austin to Berlin. Since the money was sent by light wagon and was an easy prey for highwaymen, the company purchased a new "cannonball" safe equipped with the then-newfangled time locks. All went well for a few trips, the wagon safe carrying payrolls down to Berlin and gold bars back to the company headquarters in Austin on the return trips.

Finally, when the wagon was between Berlin and Ione on its way back to Austin, it was stopped by three masked men. They did not bother to attempt opening the safe, but simply removed it intact from the wagon and rode off into the Shoshone Mountains to the east.

An intensive search for the robbers took place, but they had covered their tracks well. Eventually the safe was found where the outlaws had waited for the time locks to run their course. The bullion was gone and not enough of a trail was left to follow the robbers.

The town of Ione, at an altitude of 6800 feet, is shown as it looked around 1898, in decline. The "green house" is located on the far right end of the main street, just before the road enters the canyon leading down to Ione Valley.

At that time one of the most common forms of gold bullion were "miners' bricks." These were tiny, odd-shaped gold bars which were hand cast by miners and prospectors who melted down their own ore. Three miners living in an abandoned store in Ione maintained they were working a claim near the Shamrock Mine above town. For men hand-working a small operation, though, they suddenly seemed to have a large number of miners' bricks to spend around town. The Sheriff became suspicious and decided to visit them at home. The trio saw him coming with a few deputies, opened fire, and were killed in the resulting gunfight. The Sheriff later found evidence that they had been melting down bars stolen in the robbery, all marked with the distinctive stamp of the Nevada Stokes Company, and forming miner's bricks. Only a small portion of the stolen shipment could be accounted for, however.

Many Ione residents felt that the remainder of the gold must be hidden somewhere in the old store building. When it was finally torn down in 1937, people dug up every inch of ground under the building without success. The lumber was salvaged and a new structure, known locally as the "green house," was built on the lot. In the early 1970's, an Ione resident was cleaning out an old cellar behind the green house when he noticed a piece of metal embedded in the dirt. When dug up it proved to be an old handmade mold for small gold ingots. The rest of the cellar floor was excavated, but nothing else was recovered.

All evidence points to the highwaymen having hidden their gold somewhere around what is now the green house in Ione. Today the land is still private property, and occupied, so if anyone happens upon the gold it will probably be the owner.

The National Mine, located on the north side of Buckskin Peak. Somewhere on the south side of this mountain a high-grade gold and silver deposit is still hidden.

30. LOST BUCKSKIN MINE

Sometime in the 1890's, two Idaho prospectors were traveling eastward across northern Humboldt County enroute to Tuscarora. One night's camp found them at a small spring on the south slope of Buckskin Peak in the Santa Rosa Mountains.

The following morning one man was fixing breakfast while the other rounded up their horses to begin packing them. In collecting the frisky animals, the prospector found a ledge of rock which he did not recognize. He broke off a piece and took it along with the horses back to camp, where he showed the strange specimen to his partner. He also was at a loss to determine its composition, so he put it in his saddlebags and continued on. At Tuscarora, the rock was left at a blacksmith's for several months before it was assayed. The results were astounding—the rock running $16,000 to the ton in gold and silver.

After hurriedly outfitting, the two men returned to Buckskin Peak to locate the property. Although they searched diligently, they were never able to find the ledge which the sample had come from. They found other springs in the area and were not even sure which one they had stayed at, since they had been there just the one night. Finally they abandoned the search and passed on the story to other prospectors.

In following years the Neversweat and the Ward & Bell mines were located on the north side of Buckskin Peak. These and the mines still further north in and around the town of National produced quite a bit of ore. But these were all silver mines, all located north of the peak. The two prospectors vehemently claimed that their ore was silver and *gold* and that they had found it on the *south* side of Buckskin Peak. It is quite possible that the outcrop has been covered most of the time through the years and that a high grade deposit still remains to be found on those southern slopes of Buckskin Peak.

31. CRESCENT SPRINGS TREASURE

In 1880, when southern Nevada was still a very wild country, the *Gila*, a Colorado River steamboat, was robbed near the gold mining camp of Eldorado Canyon. The thief got away with several hundred pounds of gold and silver ingots and gold nuggets and headed off on horseback toward California. A posse tracking the outlaw found his dead packhorse at Crescent Spring, south of Nipton just inside the Nevada state line, but there was no trace of the booty. As it all weighed too much to be carried with the rider on one horse, people naturally surmised that the nuggets and ingots must have been buried somewhere in the vicinity of the spring.

Just after the turn of the century, in about 1905, discoveries in the area led to the creation of the town of Crescent, and numerous people flocked to the site. While digging a well north of the spring, one miner discovered a silver ingot from the 1880 robbery. This created a furor over the buried treasure, and people began searching for it in earnest. However, nothing more was found at that time.

Then in 1914, a couple of boys riding near the spring found a strangely-shaped rock which resembled a bar of soap. Their parents realized it was a gold ingot and sold it for enough to move "back to civilization." The unusual shape came from the fact that the early miners in Eldorado Canyon used soap molds for casting their melted bullion, thus again pointing to evidence of the 1880 theft.

No further reports of treasure have come from the Crescent district, but the known finds and the amount stolen indicate that there could well be a sizeable cache of gold and silver still hidden under the sagebrush near the spring at Crescent.

32. TUSCARORA GOLD

In 1864, seven men on a prospecting expedition from Idaho entered Nevada and began searching along the Owyhee River and then into Independence Valley. At McCann Creek they found rich placer gold, accumulating more than 200 pounds of it in short order. In the future this area would be near the mining town of Tuscarora in Elko County, but at that time the seven men were alone in the region and had to keep a constant watch out for Indians.

One day a party of Shoshones did surprise the men, who barely had time to gather about $100,000 of their gold and dig in before the attack. The prospectors quickly realized that they could not hold out indefinitely, so two men of the party were selected to ride to Silver City, Idaho, for help.

The pair of riders managed to get through the Indians and did raise a party of men to come in aid of the five men under attack. They were too late though, arriving after all five of the beseiged men had been killed. The two rescuers searched the area for the gold but could not find it.

In 1867, another group of prospectors located rich gold deposits which created Tuscarora. Among the men who came to the new strike were the two who had ridden to Idaho for help three years before. They were not interested in the gold mines, but were determined to find the already-mined gold which had been left behind during the Indian raid. They finally located one

Tuscarora, c. 1880. The pine trees lining the street are not planted, but have been placed there in pots in honor of some local celebration.

of the Shoshone who had attacked them and from him they learned that no gold had been found on or near the site of the killings. This could only mean that the five had buried it before dying.

In March, 1870, the *Elko Independent* reported that the original gold strike which the seven men from Idaho had been working in 1864, had been relocated. The news story stated the mine was eight miles northeast of the Bruno mines and was "of wonderful richness in both gold and silver."

But with all the hordes of prospectors who have combed that region in the past twelve decades, none have ever reported any hint of the buried gold. The site of the Indian seige was unknown during the Tuscarora rush, even though it must have been a good-sized camp. According to the *Independent* the prospectors "threw up breast-works and kept the savages at bay for several days, killing many of them as they charged upon the little fortification." The fortune those five men died protecting is probably still buried on or near that battlefield.

33. STAR CITY TREASURE CACHE

Located northeast of Lovelock in the Humboldt Range of eastern Pershing County, Star City was founded in 1861, the year Nevada became a Territory. A few rich mines attracted hundreds of people and within two years the community boasted the amenities of a well-established town. Hotels, saloons, banks, and stores did a booming business, supplying most of the needs of the 1200 area residents.

In June 1863, Pierre Bordreaux rode into town with the intention of staking a mining claim. He quickly found that two obstacles stood in his way. In the two years since the first discovery all the ground that could possibly contain ore had already been staked; and Bordreaux's heavy accent earned him the distrust then prevalent against foreigners.

"Frenchy" Bordreaux liked the looks of Star City, though. He had been a success as a Mississippi riverboat gambler so the problems he faced in being accepted here seemed small to him. A money belt containing $4,000 was strapped around his waist, profits from his days in the gambling salons of the paddle wheelers. If he could not become a mine owner, then he decided to find another line of business to try his hand at.

It did not take Bordreaux long to decide what to do. The first meal he ate in a Star City dining hall was so bad that he set out to try all the eateries in town in hopes of finding one he could patronize regularly. In a few days he had dined in every business in town which served food and had yet to enjoy a meal. Seeing a definite need, Bordreaux decided to open a restaurant.

He purchased a lot on Star City's main street, then hired a crew to begin erecting a building. While it was going up he rode to Winnemucca, bought out a cafe there, and freighted all the equipment to his new location. In short order his Star City Restaurant held its grand opening.

The first customers entered just for the notoriety of the new business. Many were taken aback by the steep charges, a complete dinner costing $5.00. But after one meal his reputation was made, as his food was unquestionably the best for miles around. An hour's wait to be seated soon was quite common.

Bordreaux prospered, quickly becoming an accepted member of the community. Throughout the winter of 1863-64, the restaurant did a land office business Monday through Saturday. Sunday was his day off, and whenever the weather permitted he spent time fishing in nearby streams. His angling success was such that Monday's menu usually offered the previous day's catch.

In April 1864, Oscar Sathers arrived to assume his position as superintendent of one of Star City's mills. With him were his wife and 19-year old daughter, Harriett, whom Bordreaux immediately fell in love with. In July, Harriett Sathers became Mrs. Pierre Bordreaux.

She was a big woman, standing nearly a foot taller than her husband. She was also an immediate asset to his business, aiding in reorganizing and refining the restaurant's operation. But one thing she could not change was her husband's strange banking practice. At the close of every week Bordreaux carefully divided the restaurant's proceeds exactly in two. One half was again divided and deposited in the town's two banks. The second half was wrapped and taken into the hills for hiding on his Sunday fishing trips.

It was not long before Clyde Tarpy, one of Star City's local rogues, began to take an interest in Bordreaux's finances. He nosed around very carefully and managed to befriend contacts in both banks. By comparing deposits with estimated proceeds, Tarpy soon reasoned that the Frenchman had to be hiding a good portion of the profits. But with that deduction, he seemed to have forsaken whatever good sense he may have possessed.

Instead of stalking Bordreaux to learn the location of his cache, Tarpy confronted the Frenchman in his own kitchen. He demanded to know where the money was hidden, pulling out a large caliber revolver to press his point. But Bordreaux did not scare easily. In a flash he tossed the contents of the pan he was stirring on the stove directly into the outlaw's face. Horribly burned, Tarpy still managed to fire a shot that took Bordreaux square in the chest.

Fatally wounded, the Frenchman attempted to tell his wife where his hiding place was. The bullet had punctured a lung, though, and he could only gurgle incoherently in the few minutes before he died. Tarpy was never tried for the crime, as he died within a month of blood poisoning caused by his burns.

Harriett Bordreaux, her father, and a good portion of Star City's population spent countless hours searching without success for the estimated $30,000 cache. They never found even a trace of it. Star City soon began to decline and by 1880 had been almost completely abandoned. Only Mrs. Bordreaux's recollections, written down at the close of the 19th century, preserved the story. Even so, it remains one of the least known of the state's treasure tales. Whether gold or greenbacks, Bordreaux's $30,000 is probably still hidden just off a long-abandoned trail leading from Star City to one of the Humboldt Range's fishing streams.

An early photograph of the Stewart Ranch, site of present day Las Vegas, where Mashbird stopped before his fateful prospecting trip into the McCullough Mountains.

34. TWO LOST MINES IN THE McCULLOUGH MOUNTAINS

The McCullough Mountains, southwest of present day Las Vegas, is the site of two lost mines discovered by Mormon prospectors. The first find, located by a man named Mashbird, occurred before 1900 when Las Vegas was the site of the Stewart ranch. Mashbird and a companion stopped there to refresh themselves before continuing their prospecting trip into the McCullough's. About a month later Mashbird stumbled into the ranch claiming he had been attacked by an Indian.

He said that he and his partner had camped by a spring in the mountains and prospected the surrounding country. One day an Indian entered their camp and was invited to sit down and eat. He accepted and later told the two men that he would show them where there was a large gold deposit. Mashbird went off with the Indian while his partner stayed at the camp.

On the trail the Indian maneuvered behind Mashbird and smashed him in the head with a rock, leaving him for dead. He regained consciousness, though, and stumbled along the trail a short distance further where he did find a deposit of gold. He gathered a few specimens then retraced his path until he found his campsite, but his partner had been murdered and their belongings stolen.

Suffering from his head wound, Mashbird made it back to Stewart's Las Vegas Ranch where he eventually recovered. The blow to the head and his trip through the desert had fogged his memory though, and he was never able to return to the gold.

Another story describes an unnamed Mormon prospector who arrived at the Ivanpah mill near the Nevada-California state line with a couple of burros laden with gold ore. He was very close-mouthed, sold the ore, and returned eastward into Nevada. Over a period of many months the prospector returned to the mill with identical ore, never giving a hint as to its origin, always retracing his steps into the McCullough Mountains in Nevada.

His visits abruptly stopped and some time later his body was found on the desert where he had been murdered. An abandoned camp was eventually found on the west side of the McCullough's, but it was never proven to be his and no gold was ever located. A few today still believe his deposit to be unfound and an occasional treasure seeker still searches the McCullough Mountains, combing the hills for the gold of the two Mormon prospectors.

35. DONNER PARTY TREASURE

The tragic story of the Donner Party and their ordeal in crossing the Sierra in 1846 has been thoroughly covered time and again by many history writers. A little known fact, though, has recently come to light which shows that many of the gold coins which were in the party were buried in north-central Nevada long before the wagon train ever came in sight of the Sierra.

When the Donner Party was struggling to cross the desert between Salt Lake and Nevada, many of the members began to abandon their possessions. Little by little more and more belongings were thrown away to reduce the loads for the straining draft animals until just about all that remained were necessities.

At the junction of the Reese and Humboldt Rivers, Frazier Reed and his family decided to lighten their wagon by hiding their hoard of gold coins which they had brought from the East. Though $15,000 in gold takes up little room, it weighs a considerable amount, so Reed carefully buried it next to a rock outcrop near where the two rivers meet.

Reed survived the terrible crossing of the mountains, the tragedies which followed in California, and the unease of the Civil War, but it was not until 1865 that he and his son were able to return to Nevada to fetch the buried money. Whether the topography had changed in the intervening years or his memory had failed him is not known, but to the best of the Reed family's knowledge the $15,000 in buried gold coins has never been found. It may well be still hidden near a rocky outcrop immediately north of the present site of the town of Battle Mountain.

36. MOUNTAIN SPRINGS TREASURE

In the mid 1850's, Mormons established a mining camp at Potosi, near Mountain Springs in the Spring Mountains southwest of Las Vegas. There they mined lead ore, primarily for use in making bullets, but low-yield ore and Indian troubles caused them to shut down. By 1861, the Colorado Mining Company renewed operations.

In 1897, two brothers and a mule skinner headed southwest from Utah with a wagon load of supplies and two chests holding $20,000 in silver coins for the Colorado Mining Company. Near Mountain Springs they were attacked by Indians who killed one brother outright and left the other two men for dead. A few days later they were found, seriously wounded but still alive, and were taken to the Colorado Mining Company's camp and placed in the care of a Paiute woman there. Neither recovered from their wounds, but before they died one of the men told the woman that just before the attack they had managed to hide the two chests of silver behind a rock. Later, though wounded, the two survivors were able to scrape a swallow depression in the dirt where they deposited the money.

After the two men died the Indian woman tried unsuccessfully to locate the silver. She finally told others about the treasure, and they too searched, but always without success. In this century there was much traffic through the area and even a highway was built westward through the Spring Mountains from Las Vegas to Pahrump. Today at Mountain Springs a small community consists of about 150 people and a lodge, yet no trace has ever surfaced of the nearby chests of buried silver.

View of the Truckee River Canyon just upstream from Nixon. Looking east, this photo was taken sometime in the early part of this century and shows the now-dismantled Southern Pacific Railroad spur in the foreground. The Chinese wagon train was probably bound down this canyon when they were ambushed, as this is the only major source of fresh water in the region.

37. GOLD AT NIXON

Two legends persist of 19th century caches of gold coins which are supposedly located near the town of Nixon at the south end of Pyramid Lake. The first concerns the Paiute Indian doctor Johnny Calico, who lived at the lake and is reported to have buried a sack containing gold coins on the lakeshore underneath a large rock.

The second is a tale of a group of Chinese camped at the south end of the lake in the 1860's. They were known to have carefully removed small amounts of gold from mines which had been abandoned as worthless by whites. Supposedly these Orientals had been doing this in California and had amassed enough to have it converted into two chests of gold coins.

After making camp, the Chinese were attacked by Paiutes. Wiped out to a man, their belongings were rifled for whatever the Indians wanted. At that time they had no use for white men's coins, so they abandoned the chests at the base of a cliff near the lake.

No reports of either of these treasures surfaced until 1969, when a large number of gold coins were discovered in a vacant lot across the street from the store in the present town of Nixon. Fragments of old cloth also were found with the coins, indicating that the gold may have been buried in a sack or wrapped in sacking.

At any rate, all the land in the viciniy of the town is now part of the Pyramid Lake Indian Reservation, and digging for treasure or artifacts is prohibited. The two stories have never been documented, but the fact remains that gold coins have certainly been found and more may be hidden nearby.

38. LOST LEAD-SILVER MINE

Sometime very early in this century two young men from California arrived at a village on the Humboldt River. Different versions of the tale place the town as Rye Patch or Humboldt, but the stories agree that they purchased a full complement of supplies and headed west into the desert.

Two weeks later they returned to the outfitting point, disappointed and heading back home, but carrying a piece of high-grade silver ore. They said their grandfather had headed for California during the gold rush and traveled west along the Emigrant Trail. In this area the wagon train had stopped to rest the animals and their grandfather had hunted for fresh meat. At one point he discovered what may have been a vein of lead ore and gathered some pieces of it to cast into bullets.

Though carried on to California, the ore was never melted down. Instead, one large piece was used for many years as a door

stop in a San Francisco home. One day a miner noticed the rock and persuaded the boys that it should be assayed. It was found to be rich in silver! From their grandfather's journal they figured out where the vein might be found so they set out to look for it.

For a fortnight they searched without finding any evidence of ore. Finally on the last day they happened upon the remains of an old campsite. Among the rubbish they found rock identical to the doorstop, but neither man could find indication of where the ore could have been originally discovered by their grandfather.

Many urged them to return to the desert campsite and continue searching, but the two men insisted that they had run out of time and had to return to San Francisco. They never came back to Nevada and no trace of their grandfather's lead-silver vein has ever been located.

Humboldt House, the Southern Pacific Railroad community where the two men from San Francisco probably outfitted.

TREASURE BRIEFS

The following treasure leads are included here even though further authentification has not been located. Until additional facts are brought to light, if ever, these stories must be treated as mere legend.

39 An early-day Nevada homesteader, Joshua Ward and his family were killed by Indians in 1878 at their cabin in the Ruby Mountains near the south end of Ruby Lake. So isolated was their home that the killings were supposedly not known about until distant relatives from Massachusetts came searching years later. In the family's yard they found the remains of a wagon which contained two tons of rich gold-bearing ore. Extensive searches were made for the source of the gold but no trace of it was ever located. (White Pine County)

40. During Round Mountain's heyday a local tough named Carl Flasch supposedly stole a heavy gold ingot from a mill and headed north in a buckboard. The theft was reported soon after it was committed and two deputies by the names of Bryan and Lees started in hot pursuit. The trail of the buckboard led roughly west then north through Indian Valley and into Reese River Valley. At a spot about a mile from where the Bowler Ranch meets the Reese River road, the deputies managed to shoot one of the horses pulling the light wagon. Flasch took to the brush, and in the ensuing gunfight he was killed. The gold bar was never recovered, having been disposed of along the way or concealed at or near the scene of the shootout. (Nye County)

41. Another story of stolen mill bars concerns the reported cache of several silver ingots near Treasure City. A dying man supposedly stated that they were buried "along the fence of the livery stable corral, down below the mill that is in the narrows south of Shermantown." No further documentation of this story has been located. (White Pine County)

42. Treasure City is also reputed to be the location of a cache of $3200 in gold coin. A Cornish miner decided one winter night that he wanted to go down from Treasure Hill to Shermantown to physically settle an agrument with a local bartender there. A heavy snowstorm was raging at the time, and he was advised not to try it. But he threw all his belongings into an ore sack and started into the storm. Several hours later he was found at the door of a saloon in Shermantown near death from exposure. Before he died he rambled about things like "flat rock," "under west side of big stump," "steep trail," "just below fork," and "in me billy." Since he had less than $10 on him at the time, it was supposed that he hid the remainder of his wealth along one of the foot trails leading from Treasure City to Shermantown, but none of it was ever reported found. (White Pine County)

43. In 1867, a herd of several hundred half-broke mustangs were driven into a camp in Pahranagat Valley about ten miles below Hiko. The drovers, Sam Vail and Robert Knox, were moving east to Utah to sell, but instead they stayed in the area for a few months.

Late in the summer the camp was suddenly abandoned and a half-buried saddle with the initials "R.K." burned into it was found at the site. Shortly afterwards, law officers investigating the scene located the murdered body of Robert Knox.

A warrant for the arrest of Sam Vail was forthcoming, and he was soon arrested in Austin. Once back in Hiko he was quickly tried, found guilty, and hanged, but not before he was able to write a letter to Knox's sister. In it he stated he had buried the $15,000 in cash which he and Knox owned and a cashier's check belonging to Knox in a fruit jar at the scene of the murder. The sister is reported to have searched many times for the money, but she always came up empty-handed. (Lincoln County)

44. The 19th century Columbus-Candelaria stage was once stopped by a highwayman who demanded the Candelaria payroll which it was carrying. Legend has it that the outlaw was closely pursued toward Columbus but managed to bury the loot outside of town before he was captured. Nothing further is known of the fate of the outlaw, the location of the money, or the veracity of the story. (Esmeralda County)

45. John Esterly and his three wives must have done something wrong in the eyes of the Mormon Church, because he was banished from Utah and set out on muleback toward the west. At one camp near the headwaters of the Humboldt River, it is rumored that he found high-grade ore, so rich that in Carson City it later assayed $150,000 per ton. Knowing he could not hope to return to the site without being followed, he agreed to lead a party there and share in the find. When they arrived in the same area, though, Esterly could not relocate the gold. At first his story was widely doubted, but since he continued to search time and again, though always in vain, he was eventually believed. The gold, however, was never found. (Elko County)

46. Devil's Peak, southeast of Goodsprings, is reported to be the site of a lost mine that cost the lives of five men. Supposedly, the men had located a deposit or ore running $1,000 per ton but quarreled over the division of it. A gunfight broke out and all five died in the battle. When the bodies were found there was rich ore scattered about but no clue as to the location of the deposit. (Clark County)

47 In the central Nevada mining town of Manhattan an old resident named Sam was believed to have hidden a gallon jar filled with gold and a piece of iron pipe full of silver dollars on his property. It is reported that before his death Sam told some friends that he could sit on his porch and see where his wealth was buried. His property consisted of empty lots to the west of town and three houses in a row on the town's edge. (Nye County)

48. An unsuccessful prospector named Jack Allen quit the goldfields of California to try his luck in Nevada. In a small canyon at the foot of Mt. Helen, east of the Stonewall Mountains, he picked up some rich specimens of quartz. Some days later he arrived in a mining camp, had the samples assayed, and was astounded that they returned $32,000 per ton. Allen quickly resupplied and headed back to the canyon but failed to locate it again. He eventually concluded that a flash flood during his absence had changed the terrain, so he moved on to other areas. The region is today a part of the Las Vegas Bombing and Gunnery Range. (Nye County)

49. A legend in southern Nevada concerns the buried treasure of an official of the Jackrabbit Mine at Delamar. Working in collaboration with an assayer, this man is reported to have buried some $70,000 in stolen bullion. But he died before he could make use of it and had not told the assayer where the treasure was hidden. (Lincoln County)

50. A pair of successful California miners were supposedly traveling east near Hickison Summit, where today's U.S. 50 runs, when they had a bitter quarrel. At camp that night one of the pair, unknown to his partner, buried the gold they were carrying. The next morning their argument blossomed, ending with the death of the man who had hidden the gold. The other was never able to locate it and later told friends they had camped near a site called "The Peaks," but this name is unknown today. (Lander County)

51. Still another unverified legend tells of a wagon train of successful miners laden with gold returning east from California. In northern Humboldt County they are said to have befriended a hungry Indian to whom they provided food and clothing before traveling on. A short while later the Indian spotted a war party of other Indians headed to intercept the wagon train. In return for the kindness shown him he rode back to warn the miners. Thus they had time before the attack to bury their gold, but they were subsequently wiped out and their wagons burned. It is said that an early Nevada surveyor found the burned wagons some years later and named the nearby cliff Disaster Peak. (Humboldt County)

52. Somewhere around 1910 a cowhand in eastern Humboldt County is reputed to have discovered a rich streak of gold ore. He later confided in a few friends and agreed to lead them to the spot, but was subsequently kicked in the head by a horse and killed. Before he died, the cowboy is said to have told his friends that the gold was located on Kelly Creek on the east slope of the Osgood Range. (Humboldt County)

53. Early parties of Spanish explorers are believed to have traveled through Nevada and, in a very few cases, to have worked rich surface deposits. While its existence has never been documented in any form, one such Spanish gold mine is said to have been located near Harrison Pass in the Ruby Mountains. Local Shoshone Indians are supposed to know of its location but are prevented from doing anything about it by a taboo. (Elko County)

54. John Hooley was a rancher in the Reese River Valley just south of the Lander County line. He was a big man, tall and broad, and feared nothing on earth with the possible exception of ghosts. In fact, he refused to set foot outdoors after dark. He was also an accomplished stone mason. Most of the stone and brick buildings standing today along the Reese River were built by him and he laid the first concrete sidewalks in Austin as well. He was highly paid for his expertise, and his ranch was a money maker. When he died suddenly in the 1920's, his family estimated that he should have had in excess of $60,000 saved from all his labors. Try as they would, though, they could not find any of it. Other people have searched all over his property in the intervening years, but no one has ever found a trace. (Nye County)

55. Just above the old mining camp of Ione, in the Shoshone Mountains, there were two old Spanish arrastras. The one at Ione Spring was hauled away to a ranch in the Reese River Valley many years ago, but the arrastra at Spanish Spring remained intact. Not long ago a local miner decided to hand-work the few hundred pounds of ore still stacked near the arrastra. He was quite surprised when it returned a nice showing of gold, but the most surprising thing of all was the rock itself. The miner was very familiar with the country around Ione, but had never seen this particular type of ore before. He combed the countryside trying to find the source, but never did. No one before or since has ever found paying gold ore near these springs, and the source of the ore at the old Spanish arrastra remains a mystery. (Nye County)

56. Another legend of the Shoshone Mountains tells of an old German prospector who located a seam of gold high in Knickerbocker Canyon, four miles north of Berlin. He opened the ore deposit and worked it by hand, building a well constructed cabin nearby. Legend has it that he did not like people as a rule, but loved kids. Some who visited him were most struck by the large iron cookstove he had manhandled high into the canyon, and by the fact that he kept his gold in a coffee can hidden near his home.

Upon his sudden death, of natural causes, people in the vicinity believed there to be a small fortune in gold buried near the cabin. Searches were conducted, turning up nothing of value, and the story was slowly forgotten as the area's mining camp population declined.

Then in the 1970's, a young miner living nearby heard the story and decided to investigate. After much searching he managed to locate the remains of a cabin just where the legend said the German had lived. "It was a nice one," he said, "built of lumber. But it was completely collapsed and all that remained was an old iron cookstove." He and a friend made three trips back up to the cabin to hunt for the gold, but they were as unsuccessful as all the others. (Nye County)

The main street of Searchlight, photographed around 1930. At a campsite near here a young mining engineer stumbled onto a frying pan filled with gold, its source still a mystery.

57. Near Searchlight a mining engineer happened upon an abandoned campsite while looking for a suitable place to spend the night. He decided that the previous resident had chosen a good spot and proceeded to set up his own camp there. While poking through the remains of the earlier camp, he uncovered a half-buried iron skillet filled with high grade gold ore. Searching the area, the engineer soon found a ledge of the same ore. He realized he had stumbled on a discovery which someone had located, hidden from prying eyes, and never returned for.

He carefully gathered a number of samples, covered any trace of the ore body, and in his mind fixed certain nearby points as markers. He had the samples assayed and they were rich, but after outfitting and returning to the same area he was never able to locate the objects he had chosen as markers. (Clark County)

58. The November 26, 1889 issue of the Carson City *Morning Appeal* carried a brief account of an old miner's deathbed statement. He claimed three bars of gold bullion had been buried in Silver City in 1862. It was not stated how the old-timer came to know these facts, for all he said before dying was that "they were buried in the cellar of an old ruined hotel near Devil's Gate." No report has ever come down through the years of these ingots being found. (Lyon County)

59. In September 1870, just two months before he was arrested for participating in the West's first train robbery at Verdi, noted highwayman Big Jack Davis is reported to have hidden $21,837 worth of gold coins in an outhouse in Carson City. The ill-fated train holdup landed him in the state prison to serve a ten-year sentence. Pardoned for helping to stop a prison break, Davis still could not walk the straight and narrow. Eugene Blair, a tough shotgun guard for Wells Fargo, killed him as he attempted to rob a stagecoach in 1877, and Davis was never able to recover the outhouse cache. (Carson City County)

60. In a story practically identical to that of Hardin's lost silver, John Forman was also a member of an emigrant wagon train crossing the Black Rock Desert in 1852. Like Hardin, he stumbled onto a slab of metal while out hunting for fresh meat. He, too, cut away some and cast bullets of it. Later all the bullets were used up fighting Indians on the Pit River.

Forman eventually settled in California where he finally saw a chunk of native lead that reminded him of the slab he had seen back in Nevada. With nothing better to do, and thinking that there just might be some silver in with the lead, Forman traveled back to the Black Rock country to locate the "mine." Though he searched for a number of summers he was never able to locate it again.

Idah Strobridge, in her 1904 book *In Miner's Mirage Land*, states that the find was made on "the mountain due west of, and in the next range from the one since known as Hardin Mountain." (Humboldt County)

61. A few years after the turn of the century, Peter Prengle was prospecting around Black Knob in the Humboldt Range just east of Lovelock. His burros strayed some distance during the night, while he was camped at Black Knob Spring, and he started out after them on foot the following morning. About four miles from camp, on top of a high pass, he caught up to the burros and also stumbled onto a ledge containing white quartz. He gathered some samples which he took back to camp along with the recalcitrant burros. Later panning showed the quartz to contain quite a bit of gold but Prengle was unable to relocate the ledge. (Pershing County)

62. Jim Nelson, the discoverer of the Royal Gorge mines which created the camp of Omco in eastern Mineral County, was not satisfied with the wealth his discoveries gave him. In 1917 he was back prospecting the country between the Athens district and Pactolus when he happened onto some extremely rich float. Select specimens assayed as high as $40,000 per ton but nowhere could Nelson find a trace of the parent vein. For the rest of his life he combed the area, sometimes finding additional pieces of the float, but never its source. (Nye County)

110

63. On August 6, 1926, Allen A. Bruce stole $34,000 in currency from a government payroll shipment in Susanville, California. He first buried the money near the site of the theft, later retrieving it and burying it in various locations in and around Reno. When he was arrested all but $12,000 was accounted for. Bruce told authorities that he had carefully wrapped the bills in sections of rubber inner tubes and buried the bundle on a hillside near Reno Hot Springs (now the River Inn) west of Reno. He attempted to lead law officers to the site to recover the money but was unable to locate it again. Federal Judge Farrington refused to grant him additional time to look for the money, instead fining Bruce $12,000 and sentencing him to 30 months in federal prison. An accomplice, James Smith, also failed in his attempts to show the authorities where the loot was, and he received a fine of $10,000 and a sentence of 20 months. No evidence indicated that either man ever recovered the money later. (Washoe County)

64. In 1916, prospector John Durkin found some pieces of very rich and extremely unusual float in a canyon near the north end of Pyramid Lake. The ore consisted of a combination of gold, silver, and mercury all contained in a "brownish" rock. Durkin found numerous pieces of the float as he searched for the vein it originated from, even sinking a total of 400 feet of exploratory trenches and tunnels. One large boulder, weighing close to a ton, carried a two-inch seam of the ore along one side. It could not have traveled any great distance from the vein as the ore was extremely brittle, breaking if dropped from shoulder height, yet Durkin was never able to find the source. By today's prices, the lowest assay on the ore showed it contained $13,000 in silver, $1,800 in gold, and $163 of mercury to the ton. (Washoe County)

65. An 80-pound bar of gold bullion is reported to be still buried somewhere just off the old Bodie to Carson road between Wellington and Walley's. Milton Sharp, the infamous Nevada stage-robber who is said to have held up five Wells Fargo treasure coaches in the summer of 1880 alone, lifted an entire shipment of these bars off a Carson Mint-bound stage while his nemesis, shotgun messenger Mike Tovey, was recuperating from wounds. Sharp was soon arrested in San Francisco and all but one of the bars was recovered where he had buried them. He received a sentence of twenty years in the Nevada State Prison, but after his release neither his appearance nor his style of living indicated that he ever retrieved the ingot. (Douglas County)

66. A large number of pieces of float, containing "tellurium" gold ore, were found in the Farrel district about seven miles north of Seven Troughs. One large specimen, weighing several pounds and held together with iron straps, was exhibited at the Lewis and Clark Exposition in 1904. The Stall brothers leased the Myers property in the hopes of locating the source of the rich float, but in years of exploration they failed to discover the main ore body. They eventually gave the property back to Charles Myers who searched for the vein diligently, but unsuccessfully, until his death in 1926. High grade float is still found occasionally in the area, but its source remains hidden. (Pershing County)

67. A stone-cutter and prospector named William Lindsey once found a vein of gold in the mountains west of the Comstock Lode. He gathered enough ore samples to be able to pile them in a pyramid to have a photograph taken. The find was not recorded though, as Lindsey believed the ground where it was located to be land owned by the railroad. Instead, he carefully covered over the vein to keep it secret. When he finally found out the land was free and could be staked upon, he was unable to again find the outcrop. The location is said to be in what is known as the Big "D" district, visible from Carson City, and covered by a "malapi flow." (Near junction of Storey, Washoe, and Carson City Counties)

68. Three Carson City residents, Sam Wright, Charles Brey, and Charles Witheral, owned and worked a mine in the Carson Range above Genoa during the 1870's. The ore contained a mixture of gold, silver, and copper but proved to be uneconomical to mill due to its complexity and the then-low prices of silver and copper. The mine was shut down for some years until the value of copper and silver made it feasible to reactivate it. But when the three men went out to reopen the property, they could not find it. Either a landslide or avalanche had swept down the hillside and removed all indication of the mine's location.

On his deathbed, Witheral gave a map of the mine and many pounds of ore samples to Hal Lemmon. Though he and his friends searched for years, they were also unable to find the mine and it remains hidden to this day. (Douglas County)

69. A French Canadian named Duckett is reported to have set out from Belmont in 1871, intending to prospect along the Colorado River. He later said he passed through Stone Cabin Valley and reached Black Mountain near Thirsty Canyon. Here an Indian met him and offered to lead him to a rich gold deposit in trade for one of Duckett's horses. The prospector agreed, and was soon led to a ledge of high grade gold. While the Indian rode off on his new horse, Duckett gathered a sackful of the ore. Five days after leaving, he again rode into Belmont brandishing the gold-bearing quartz. For years afterward Duckett is said to have searched for the gold, but never finding it again. The location is reported to be in the vicinity of Gold Meadows near Black Mountain, 23 miles east of Scotty's Junction. (Nye County)

70. Around the turn of the century an old Douglas County Indian, known as Paiute Johnny, used to make periodic trips to Genoa to do his shopping. Whether he traded at Thompson's, Raycraft's, or some other establishment, he always paid for his purchases with specimens of rich gold ore. Numerous times men were sent to follow him in the hopes of finding the source of his gold, but no one managed to outwit the cagey Indian. When Paiute Johnny died the secret of his gold went with him, and all anyone ever knew of the deposit's location was that it was in the Pinenut Mountains across the valley to the southeast from Genoa. (Douglas County)

71. Another lost mine in the Pinenut Range lies somewhere near the top of Red Canyon near Mountain House. Ex-Surveyor General A. C. Pratt was prospecting the area when he happened to break up a rock that was streaked with gold. He searched all the rest of that afternoon and finally found what he believed was the ledge the float had come from. Pratt tied a handkerchief to a nearby bush to mark the spot but when he returned some days later he could not locate the outcrop. A band of sheep had passed through the area while he was gone and had obliterated the handkerchief and any trace of the gold-bearing ledge. (Douglas Co.)

72. A stage robbery in Stone Cabin Valley, on the Tybo to Belmont road, may have resulted in the burial of an express treasure box nearby. An eyewitness to the robbery stated that the highwaymen removed the box from the stage and carried it into a cut where the road passed through a small ridge. A few minutes later the robbers rode away, but without any sign of the loot. Perhaps the box was buried there, the outlaws intending to return for it later. It may well still be there, as highwaymen did not have long life expectancies in early Nevada. (Nye County)

73. A well-known lost mine legend states that two prospectors happened to be examining near Tonopah a mountain that had a vertical face on one side. About 500 feet from the top they spotted an area of mineralization. They carefully managed to climb down to it and were rewarded with the discovery of a vein of rich gold. By slow and painstaking work the two men were able to carve out a narrow shelf where they built a tiny cabin. When winter set in they were well supplied and were prepared to spend the months picking away at their vein. One snowy night their luck came to an end when an avalanche swept down the cliff, carrying the narrow trail, the cabin, and both men to the rocks far below. It is said that a third man also died attempting to scale the cliff to reach the site of the cabin. If this cliff-side deposit is ever relocated, getting to the gold may be even more difficult than finding it. (Nye County)

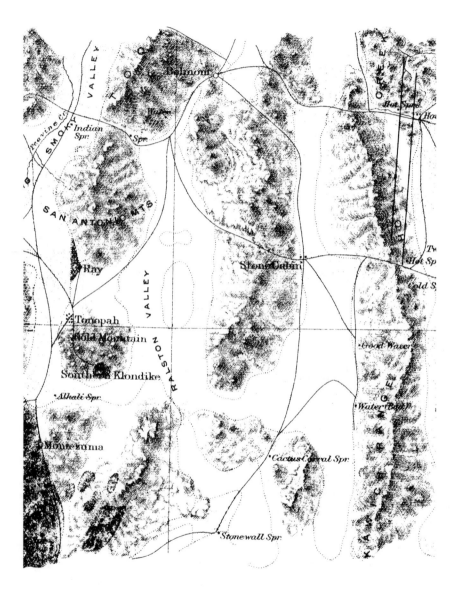

117

LEGENDS PROVEN FALSE

While the tales in this book are left for the reader to accept or reject, there are two famous accounts which recently have been proven false. To keep others from wasting time and money on a treasure which does not exist, the accounts are included here.

In both stories, research into old files, through stacks of newspapers, and into historic volumes has determined the difference between fact and fiction. Such research is the key to solving any riddle of history. It is especially important in treasure stories where just a little time and effort may literally be worth its weight in gold.

MANUEL GONZALES' BURIED LOOT

The legend of the great stage robbery at Empire and of the strongbox of gold bullion buried there, has prompted countless searchers to expend time and money hunting all over that region. Unfortunately, as research has proven, this is one treasure which is just not there.

Sometime in the 1880's, as the story went, a Pioneer Stage Company's treasure coach was making its usual run from Virginia City to Carson City. At a point just east of Empire, while the coach was passing through an area of tall sagebrush, four well-armed masked men stepped from hiding and stopped the coach. They quickly removed the strongbox and sent the stage racing toward Carson.

As soon as the story of the holdup could be told to the county Sheriff, a posse was formed and galloped out to the site of the robbery. The highwaymen had hidden their horses at a ranch on the Carson River and were still on foot trying to reach them when the posse caught up with them. In the ensuing gunfight three of the robbers were killed. The fourth, Manuel Gonzales, was captured with a slight wound. The strongbox was not recovered, though, as the outlaws had buried it along the way.

Gonzales was tried, convicted, and sentenced to a stretch in the Nevada State Prison in Carson. He served seven years, refusing to divulge the location of the gold, although he claimed he could see where it was buried from his cell window. After seven years, he contracted tuberculosis and was pardoned so that he could die on the outside. Wells Fargo also wanted him out in the hopes that he might lead them to the missing strongbox.

Once free, Gonzales made no move to recover the treasure but took a job as a handyman and janitor in a Carson butcher shop. After quite some time the butcher and his son were able to talk the old outlaw into disclosing to them where the strongbox was in return for the kindness they had shown him.

On the appointed day everything was in readiness when the old Mexican became ill and died, having suffered a stroke. The butcher, and later many residents of Carson City, searched vainly for the hidden treasure which is supposed to be buried north of the Nevada State Prison.

Now for the truth. In 1870, the Virginia & Truckee Railroad was completed between Carson and Virginia City. By the time of the 1880's, Wells Fargo had stopped sending treasure by stagecoach along this route in preference to the tighter security of the V&T's express cars. In fact, that railroad was the only one in the West that ever had a car built specifically for the transportation of gold and silver bullion. With that kind of protection, Wells Fargo would have been foolish to trust their shipments to flimsy coaches.

There are no records at the Nevada State Prison which show that a Manuel Gonzales was ever sentenced from Carson City, and the only man by that name ever sent up for robbery was from an entirely different part of the state. Wells Fargo's records, as well, show no mention of a robbery this large in the Carson area and have no data at all to give any basis to the story. One further check through the state's records of pardons and paroles show no mention of a Manuel Gonzales being set free anytime in the 19th century.

It made a good story, but unfortunately there is no strongbox full of gold and silver buried near Empire.

HANK KNIGHT'S LOST CAVE of GOLD

Hank Knight's lost gold-lined cave has long been considered one of Nevada's most prominent treasure tales. People have searched for it for many decades, but recent newspaper research has definitely proven the story false, and it can now be removed from the treasure hunter's list.

The story is supposed to have begun in 1880, when an old prospector named Henry "Hank" Knight was on a prospecting trip between the towns of Sand Springs and Painted Hills, in eastern Churchill County. Somewhere in the range of mountains between these two communities he found a rock outcrop carrying some gold. He started sinking a prospect shaft but had only gotten down a few feet when the bottom fell out and he found himself in a large cave.

Looking around, as the story goes, he discovered that the walls and floor were covered with gold. Knight took samples of the ore and headed for Sand Springs after carefully hiding all traces of the shaft and cave.

Once there, Knight showed some samples to various people. But before anything could be done about the spectacular find, the old prospector mysteriously died. A search for the cave was organized, but never met with any success and the story was forgotten. Then in 1933, George Forbes relocated the cave much as Knight had done. He secured a grubstake, started out into the mountains to begin development, and was never seen again, leaving the legend to multiply.

Research finally uncovered the true story of the cave and proved the treasure legend false. To begin with, there never was any town called Painted Hills, and Sand Springs was never more than a station for freighters and stages. With the beginning of the story already proven wrong, it seemed logical that the rest also would be untrue. That soon proved to be so.

In the September 23, 1933, issue of the *Fallon Eagle,* an article stated that George Forbes, of Fallon, had optioned the cave from its owners, Anna Cassels and Fred Olzog. He had plans to develop the property which consisted of a cave some 40 feet wide, of indeterminable length, and some three to four feet in height.

As to the discovery of the cave the *Eagle* stated, "Hank Knight, well known prospector of this section who is now with W. D. Moody near Placerville, California, . . . broke into the . . . cave years ago after completing a fifty foot shaft. Considerable ore was said to have been taken out at that time."

Thus Hank Knight had not died at Sand Springs and George Forbes did not disappear into the mountains. The cave was well known and was not owned by Forbes but by other parties. And what of the legendary ore? The *Eagle* claimed that the ore in 1933 was running about $4 a ton in gold, or about one-fifth ounce to every 2,000 pounds of rock. This is certainly not very much to build an enduring legend around.

WAGONLOAD of CONFEDERATE SILVER

While this legend has never been published as being a factual treasure story, there have been a few fictional accounts and the motion picture *Virginia City* which centered around the theme of an entire wagon of Comstock silver being highjacked by Southern sympathizers during the Civil War. The stories tell of a group of the rebels, known locally as the "Knights of the Golden Circle," who steal the silver and attempt to freight it south through the Nevada deserts. The eventual disposition of the silver varies with each version of the story, though at least one account infers that the silver was buried when the Rebs realized they could not hope to escape south into territory friendly to them.

There is absolutely no historical basis for this tale, although some verbal accounts have recently begun to circulate. Since Southern sympathizers were dealt with quite harshly in heavily pro-Union Nevada, it would have been impossible for a band of them to have spirited a stolen shipment out of the territory.

EPILOG

DANGERS of the TONGUE-IN-CHEEK TREASURE

On February 11, 1880, the following story appeared in the *Reno Evening Gazette.* It was obviously a partly-true, partly-fiction piece which early editors delighted in publishing as straight news during otherwise dull times. However, neither the dates nor the sequence of events seem plausible in view of Washoe Valley's early history.

The danger lies in the possibility that some writer or story-teller may report this otherwise harmless tale as truth, indicating that $85,000 is still buried today in the hills above Franktown.

The 1880 story is reprinted here in its entirety, both to show how easily erroneous treasure stories get started and as a humorous example of 19th century literary license.

HIDDEN TREASURE.

———

Franktown in a Blaze of Excitement.

———

$85,000 Buried By a Highwayman—
Efforts to Find the Sack of Money—
What the Spirits Say About the Matter—
History of the Search.

———

(From our own Correspondent.)

For the past few days Franktown has been the scene of a great excitement over a supposed hidden treasure. Men, women and children have been hunting in the mountains for it. The story about the treasure has been known here for the past twenty-five years. It is as follows: Some time in 1850 a man was tried and convicted of murder. Before his execution he made a confession, of which this is the substance:

THE ROBBER'S STORY.

I had been a highway robber on the plains for years and had accumulated eighty-five thousand dollars. I started back to California to take a steamer for the East. In November I reached

Washoe Valley, and seeing that a storm was brewing, I feared that I could not cross the mountains to California, so concluded to bury my money. I therefore buried it, back of Franktown, above what is known as the old Mormon mill, with the intention of returning for it in the spring. Not being satisfied with my gains, I went on the road again. Now here I stand, convicted of murder and doomed to die.

Early Search for the Gold.

The above story is as told to me by a man who heard it, and who came to Washoe valley on purpose to seek the buried treasure. He came in 1858 or '9 and was well known to your correspondent and to all the old settlers in the valley. Failing in his search, he left in disgust for parts unknown. For years nothing has been openly said about the treasure, although it has been searched for from time to time by several parties.

The Aid of Spirits Invoked.

It has been known here for several days that a prominent spiritualist from California, not at all acquainted with this section of the country, has described the exact location of the Morgan [sic] mill, and that he has led many up the side of the mountain to look after a fortune. Your correspondent has had an interview with Mrs. Bowers, "the Washoe Seeress," and she says there is treasure hidden somewhere near Franktown. As she was here in '54, she remembers well the story about the treasure. But strange to say, when she calls on her spirit friends, none of them are able to tell her the exact locality of the deposit. Even her deceased husband and brother, whom she claims to be her constant companions, say they know nothing about it. The spiritual Mr. Bowers tells her that if he did, he would be sure to tell her, as he knows she needs money.

Finding the Hole.

Maurice May had an idea that he knew where the treasure was hidden. So about 5 o'clock last Sunday morning, he and a confidential friend started out with pick and shovel to become suddenly rich. They at last reached the proper place to dig when, lo and behold, there they found a hole about four feet deep, and all that remained of the treasure was a dollar and a half, lying on the ground near the hole, an evidence that some one had been before them in the search. On the way home Maurice looked so disappointed to think that some of our Franktown Christians had robbed him of Eighty-Four Thousand, Nine Hundred and Ninety-Eight Dollars and fifty cents that a favorite dog failed to recognize him. The dog bit him and May shot the animal. It is hinted around that May suspects Judge Harcourt and Constable Frank Wooten of robbing him of the treasure that was as good as his, so that a double duel may soon be expected.

Chuck-a-Luck.

Franktown, Feb. 10, 1880.

INDEX

127